# X-Urbanism

# X-Urb

# anism

## ARCHITECTURE AND THE AMERICAN CITY

MARIO GANDELSONAS

Princeton Architectural Press     New York

Published by
**Princeton Architectural Press**
**37 East 7th Street**
**New York, NY 10003**
**1 212 995 9620**

For a free catalog of books, call 1 800 722 6657
Visit our website at www.papress.com

ISBN 1-56898-151-1
First edition
9 8 7 6 5 4 3 2 1

To Diana

Produced by Asia Pacific
Printed in China
Cover design: Sara E. Stemen
Design: Dieter Janssen
Copy editor: Beth Harrison
Research assistant: Alexander Schweder

*Special thanks to:*
*Eugenia Bell, Caroline Green, Clare Jacobson,*
*Therese Kelly, Mark Lamster, Jane Garvie, and*
*Annie Nitschke of Princeton Architectural Press*
*–Kevin C. Lippert, Publisher*
*Princeton Architectural Press*

Library of Congress
Cataloging-in-Publication Data
Gandelsonas, Mario
  **X-urbanism: architecture and the American city /**
  **Mario Gandelsonas**
  p. cm.
  Includes bibliographical references.
  ISBN 1-56898-151-1
  1. Space (Architecture) — United States.
  2. City planning — United States.
  I. Title.

NA9053.S6G36  1999
711'.4'0973022–dc21                    98-20234
                                CIP

# Contents

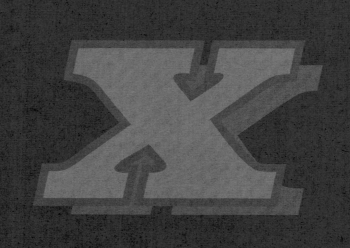

# Introduction

This book presents a project that started fifteen years ago: the project of reading the American city through drawings.[1] This exploration developed at a time when a drastic urban restructuring was taking place in the United States, a change as powerful as the suburbanization of the 1950s. In the last twenty-five years, major shifts have affected the city and urban culture, expanding their definitions, generating new configurations of urban space and form, and producing different conditions of urban viewing. The continuing development of the city and the decline of established urban spaces and public places were paralleled by the emergence and proliferation of new interior, exterior, physical, and electronic public spaces. However, in contrast to this multiplication of urban situations, this was also a time when the possibilities for an *urban architecture* in America seemed more remote than ever before.[2]

This examination of the American city was at the same time a reflection on architecture. My *urban drawings* were an attempt to depict the architectural implications of the strange metropolis that began to develop in America in the 1970s and 1980s, a process that still continues and that is now spreading to the rest of the world.[3] The drawings, by venturing into nonarchitectural territory (the city), embody an attempt to explore the limits of architecture at a time when the practice was also undergoing traumatic changes.[4] In the 1970s, the question of a critical practice of architecture, defined as the articulation between the practice and the theory of architecture, came to the foreground of the architectural debate. These discussions, centered on issues concerning urbanism, questions of meaning, and a critique of representation, were framed within the poststructuralist discourse.[5]

The urban drawings were developed in this context, as a critique of the traditional role of drawings as representations of the city as a physical fact: they were proposed as a site where the articulation of two different practices, of two different "discursive surfaces" — architecture and the city — took place. This is a difficult articulation between two mutually contradictory practices that, as I will discuss, requires complex strategic negotiation. This articulation attempts neither to fill a void, since architecture and the city have been related in different ways at different times, nor to "resolve" the antagonism between the two practices. It is rather an attempt both to recognize their differences and the necessity of their articulation, not as a fixed connection between two elements, but as a relation between two changing practices. In fact, one should see architecture and the city as signifiers pinned to two practices that have been constantly changing through time. And since the terms of the relationship between architecture and the city have been constantly changing, their connection needs to be constantly recreated and negotiated without ever achieving a definitive balance. The articulatory practice, by suggesting alternative strategies for establishing new modes of relationships, aims to further alter the identities of both urban and architectural practices.[6]

My work did not look directly at the contemporary urban condition but started with an examination, through drawings, of two cities that

---

1. I will use of the term "America" in a restricted sense to designate the United States of America.

2. The development of what is called "the new Urbanism," in my view, confirms, not contradicts, this statement. See the section called "Rewriting the City" in chapter three.

3. In fact the latest form of this city transcends national frontiers paralleling the global economy. See the example of the new cities in Southeast Asia,

in particular, the Pudong development area in China's Shanghai, and Shenzhen in the Pearl River Delta.

4. I borrow the term "traumatic" from psychoanalysis to designate events in the history of the city that are defined by their intensity, by the incapacity of the existing urban configurations to deals with them and their restructuring effects in the city. See Robert Venturi's *Complexity and Contradiction in Architecture* (New York: Museum of Modern Art,

1990) and Aldo Rossi's *The Architecture of the City* (Cambridge, Mass.: The MIT Press, 1982) might be seen as the obvious background. However, the work stems directly from Diana Agrest's early writings. See Agrest, *Architecture from Without* (Cambridge, Mass.: The MIT Press, 1992).

were "left behind" by the latest urban restructuring: New York and Los Angeles, the early-twentieth-century city and the postwar city, respectively, both acting now as two historical backgrounds against which the new contemporary city is developing. The drawings suggested questions that generated both drawings of other American cities and the need for a double theoretical examination: the emerging questions were not just about the nature of the American city[7] but also about the practice of architecture itself, not just about the object but also about the subject of the inquiry.

Most attempts to theorize American urban development present it as a process of continuous growth. Economists and planners who find their object in the flows of capital and in urban policy do not look into the formal aspects of the process. Historians and urbanists interested in those formal aspects tend to see the city as a continuous process of accretion and/or transformation where buildings are added or replaced and where public spaces are carved or built.[8] This view obscures the *formal discontinuities* in that process, the radical reconfigurations of the American city that are brought to the foreground by the object of this text: the articulation of architecture and the city.[9]

Two texts suggested the first building blocks of the urban theory presented in the first part of this book: John Reps's *The Making of the Urban America*[10] and Manfredo Tafuri's "The Enchanted Mountain" in *The American City*.[11] They represent, respectively, the philological view of the American urban historian and the critical view of the European architectural historian. When brought together, Reps and Tafuri suggest two distinct and specifically American urban formations that I will call the "gridded city" and the "city of skyscrapers." The first designates the predominant configuration of the American urban plan, and the second indicates the development of a city with a dense and compact fabric not subject to sectional constraints. A third city will be described as a radical break with respect to these two "walking cities" — a car-dependent "suburban city" with a new type of scattered fabric, the effects of which are depicted by Robert Venturi and Denise Scott Brown in *Learning from Las Vegas* (which could be considered the first architectural reading of the American city by an American architect).[12]

Besides the tendency to conceal discontinuities, the other problem of most theories is the viewing of Europe and America as fully constituted identities engaged in a stable, ahistorical, oppositional structure where each side complements the other: Europe versus America, colonial empire versus the colonized, dominant versus subordinated, old versus new, etc. This view obscures the complex process through which the identities of the European and American cities are constantly restructured. Tafuri, in his description of the 1923 Chicago Tribune Building competition entries, shows an important moment in the historical process where the urban identities of cities on both sides of the Atlantic enter a crisis. In a reversal of the centuries-long relationship of domination, the European architects have to struggle to resolve

5. See Mario Gandelsonas, "On Reading Architecture," in *Progressive Architecture* (March 1972), and Diana Agrest, "Designed versus Non-designed," in *Oppositions* 5.

6. I am paraphrasing and displacing Ernesto Laclau and Chantal Mouffe's definition of articulatory practices in *Hegemony and Socialist Strategy* (London and New York: Verso, 1985), 189.

7. However, the point from which I was "reading" the urban plans was located in the contemporary city, in the American city of the end of the twentieth century.

8. See Leonardo Benevolo, *The History of the City* (Cambridge, Mass.: The MIT Press, 1980); Pierre Lavedan, Jeanne Hugueney, and Philippe Heurat, *Urbanisme a l'Epoque Moderne*, XVI–XVIII (Paris: Art et Metier Graphiques, 1982).

9. See Saskia Sassen, *The Global City* (Princeton, N.J.: Princeton University Press, 1991); Manuel Castells, *The Informational City: Information Technology, Economic Restructuring, and the Urban-Regional Process* (Oxford: Blackwell, 1989).

10. John Reps, *The Making of Urban America* (Princeton, N.J.: Princeton University Press, 1965).

the design of a new American urban type that challenges the centuries-old conception of the city, a situation denied by a condescending view of American architecture as too young, or nonexistent.[13]

What the standard view misses is the interdependence of the European and the American city in a transatlantic flow where the constant circulation of shapes was produced by mutual imaginary identification. This was a strange exchange, the one between two overlapping circuits of desire, in which each side identified with an image representing what it would like to be, an exchange that ultimately distorted the circulating urban configurations. For instance, the American colonial cities are described, in Reps's book, in terms of the unavoidable influence of the settlers original European cultures (Spanish, French, English, Dutch, and Swedish) and of the inevitable metamorphosis resulting from their encounter with the specific opportunities and requirements of the American environment.[14] However, what Europe brings to America at the beginning of a process of production of identity that continues today are the "ideal" urban plans that could not be implemented in the old world. The American city is not imported from Europe, but will become in fact an experimental laboratory where Europe will develop its urban fantasies. Another example can be found in the way in which the symbolic value of the European monumental axes is radically transformed when displaced to Washington, D.C. In this new situation, they not only represent a link between *democratic* institutions, but are at the same time overlapped onto a gridded plan that organizes a field of objects. The reverse transformation takes place when the American city is fantasized by Le Corbusier in the 1920s and transformed in the extruded sections proposed in his *Ville Contemporaine* of 1925.

In the first chapter, the American city emerges as a multitude of realities that include not only the plurality and diversity of U.S. cities, but also the influence of many European centers —during the colonial times and after American independence — in a constant flow of political, economic, cultural, and formal exchanges with the Americas.[15] But there is also another American city, a city present in the European Imaginary that acquires different configurations and roles. This is the American city as it appears in the architectural urban fantasies, particularly in the architectural Imaginary at the end of the nineteenth and beginning of the twentieth century. These urban fantasies will travel back to America and will be materialized in new ways, as in Le Corbusier's final version of the United Nations building in New York City or in Mies van der Rohe's American skyscrapers after World War II.[16]

While the coordinates of space that define the American city are given by the transatlantic relations between America and Europe, the coordinates of time are defined by the specific nature of the temporal dimension of the urban processes in the New World. The necessary permanence of the plan as opposed to the contingent impermanence of its fabric takes place in the chronological range of the "long duration."[17]

11. Giorgio Ciucci, Mario Manieri Elia, Francesco Dal Co, and Manfredo Tafuri, *The American City: From the Civil War to the New Deal* (Cambridge, Mass.: The MIT Press, 1979). There is a unifying hypothesis in *The American City* — the great apocalypse of European bourgeois culture — that links the four different essays. Their aim is "to critically update the historical study of the American society." The articles depict the American city as an "enormous form-defying product of technique."

12. Robert Venturi, Denise Scott Brown, and Steven Izenour, *Learning from Las Vegas* (Cambridge, Mass.: The MIT Press, 1972). See also Venturi, *Complexity and Contradiction in Architecture*. It is architectural in the sense that it is a text written by an architect and not just implied in a project.

13. Ciucci, et al., *The American City*.

14. Benevolo's *The History of the City* is one of the most blatant examples of Eurocentrism: the American city is included in a chapter called "European Colonization."

15. Fernand Braudel, *A History of Civilizations* (New York: Penguin Books, 1995); see also Tzvetan Todorov's *La decouverte de l'amerique* (Paris: Ed. du Seuil, 1972) for the question of America as the European "other."

These coordinates of space and time define the American city as a site where experiments with urban form take place, generating the traumatic changes that result in different formal structures. An example of this is the X-Urban city, the latest restructuring of the American city where the "formless" in the plan seems to dominate, where architectural concerns stop at the level of the building, and where the urban forces resist any attempts to see architectural form imposed. The emphasis seems to have shifted from the spatial dimension, where the ordering devices have been substantially impoverished, to the temporal dimension, where new and complex ordering structures have been introduced. A symptom of this situation is the fact that there is a lot more experimentation in the World Wide Web as public sphere than in the "reality" of urban space.

These urban experiments have always been related in many different ways to a second site, one where architectural research takes place in the form of the discourse and the practice of architecture. The first chapter locates the traumatic changes that produce varied formal structures in relation to these spatial and temporal coordinates in the flow back and forth from Europe to America, from the city to architecture, and depicts the traces left by these processes in the plans of the American city.

The second chapter focuses on the question of the identity of the American city or, rather, on the incomplete and open character of its identity.[18] Urban identity presupposes, among other things, an order imposed onto the configuration of the city. However, there is always a certain precariousness to this order that ultimately fails to domesticate urban form. This failure is due in part, to the resistance to fixity presented by the constantly changing economic, political, and cultural forces that traverse the city.

The break that separates the colonial from the post-Revolutionary cities of the Union produces critical changes in the urban configuration. This constitutive moment started a process of differentiation with respect to the European city where each of the three American cities discussed as moments in the "transatlantic flow" (the gridded city, the city of skyscrapers, and the suburban city) attempts to project an urban fantasy, an order that articulates the urban configurations in a new way. First, the grid, as the most powerful attempt to project an image of order throughout a continent, creates a two-dimensional diagram, and asserts the preeminence of the plan as the space where equality is represented. Second, the skyscraper attempts to reify the freedom of the individual building within the logic of capital through a cluster of differential features that organize the section. Third, the interstate highway attempts to introduce a fluidity of movement that would transform the entire territory into a field, as the signifier of a metaphorical garden where an order of oppositions — suburbs/center city, residence/workplace — is supposed to domesticate the antagonisms that traverse the American society. Each of them represents a failed attempt to establish an urban and architectural order. The grid fails to satisfy the required high densities when

---

16. As equally important as these buildings are as isolated architectural events is the influence of modernist architecture in both North and South America, which is materialized in simplified versions of the architectural models.

17. Fernand Braudel, "Histoire et sciences sociales, la longue durée," *Annales* (October–December 1958). Braudel develops the notion of "long duration" in an article written less for historians than for social scientists. The article deals with the multiplicities of time and in particular with the notion of *long duration*, of the slow time, of that which apparently does not change, with the permanences of language, of knowledge, of roads and cities, as opposed to the *short time*, which is attentive to the individual and the event.

18. In treating this subject I am extending and displacing the question of identity as it has been discussed and developed in the last decade in political theory of the urban problematic. These discussions have brought an awareness of the complex mechanism through which all identity is constructed. See Ernesto Laclau, ed., *The Making of Political Identities* (London and New York: Verso, 1994).

simply extruded in the manner of the European city. When fractured and distorted by geography and history, the skyscraper fails to become a stable architectural type because of its indifference to plan. Finally, the continental garden is traversed by freeways, an "autistic" mechanism that fails to relate either to the city or to architecture.

The third chapter maps the conceptual space in which the urban drawings were developed. The text returns to the central questions overlooked by the standard theories: that the relationship between the European and the American city was always overdetermined by another flow, the one between architecture and the city; and that the circulation of urban shapes — repeated, transformed, or mutated — was paralleled by the circulation of architectural shapes that are analogically displaced, transformed, or invented.

To fully understand the role of architecture, we have to consider not just the urban interventions, most of which take place in Europe, but also the role of architectural discourse, and not just what is being said but also the silences, the misreadings, and suppressions. This relationship between the city and architecture should actually be considered as constitutive of architecture.[19] The starting moment in the history of this relationship, and of its effects on both the city and architecture, takes place in the first renaissance architectural text, Alberti's *Ten Books of Architecture*, a text that projects an urban fantasy that will not be realized in Europe but in America, and only there in a fragmented way.[20] Since Alberti, a number of rewritings have taken place,

from Palladio through Ledoux to Le Corbusier, where the city in question is not longer Rome but the American city, seen as an immature city that is not fully developed. With every one of these rewritings the practice of architecture is altered, sometimes in radical ways. Ultimately the questions asked here, exposing the relationships between architecture and the city,[21] represent another iteration in this history of the impossible pursuit of the city as an object of architectural desire.

The American city was always seen from Europe, most times in a subordinate relation to the European city.[22] This relationship of subordination also functions with respect to the discourse of architecture. For instance, one could say that most of the narrative on the American city describes it as a source of technical innovations that influences the architecture that happens to develop in Europe, rather than as an integral part of the development of Western architecture. The rule in this narrative is the reference to the absence of architecture in the American city but also, and more importantly, to the absence of the American city in architecture.[23] This status of cultural dependency started to change only after World War II. In architectural culture, the dependent relationship changed only in the 1970s with the exchanges that occurred at the Institute for Architecture and Urban Studies in New York City when younger European architects began coming to the United States. In the last few years, the question of the American influence in Europe has been increasingly examined and developed in European academic circles.[24]

19. This relation has been constantly restructured throughout history according to changes both in the city and in architecture.

20. Leon Battista Alberti, *The Ten Books of Architecture* (reprint, New York: Dover, 1986).

21. The questions also uncover the impossibility for architecture itself of ever achieving a fixed, closed identity.

22. A typical example is Benevolo's *The History of the City*.

23. As Aldo Rossi said in his *Scientific Autobiography* (Cambridge, Mass.: The MIT Press, 1981), 75–6: "I realized at a certain point that the official criticism of architecture had not included America or, what was worse, had not looked at it: the critics were preoccupied only with seeing how modern architecture had

been transformed or applied in the United States." Venturi's theory, exposed in *Complexity and Contradiction in Architecture*, a polemical position against the canon of modernist architecture and urbanism, is the first American architectural theory to be considered by European criticism.

The architecture of the city has traditionally been produced through urban fantasies realized in drawings that attempt to impose an architectural order to the urban body. The urban drawings presented here displace the scene of production to the site of architectural reception and approach the city as a "ready-made"; the city itself becomes as a point of departure for their development.[25] The architectural nature of the urban drawing differs from the mapping activity described by Michel de Certeau[26] as one of the polities of the practice of the city: the map of the geographer versus the trajectory of the ordinary people, the same people for whom Kevin Lynch proposed a systematic approach to the image of the city.[27] Why are the drawings different? Because our object is the architecture of the city, described by our two- or three-dimensional drawings based on plans, as opposed to the phenomenological mapping suggested by Kevin Lynch. Because the urban drawings are conceived as part of a practice with the potential to transform or mutate the city and not the city as a place for the development of everyday life tactics.

Why are we interested in the plan more than in the physical reality of the city? The city is the result of a multiplicity of processes, physical and social, it is an economic dynamo that produces a physical landscape as scene of the sociopolitical play of forces, marked by and influencing those forces. The immediate questions raised for an urban observer by its configuration are related to the communicational capacity and power of these shapes and their legibility. What this perceptual surface obscures and the plan reveals is the textual and symbolic power of the city which is the register where the articulation with architecture takes place.

Part 2 of this book presents the urban drawings developed between 1984 and 1994 of New York City, Los Angeles, Boston, New Haven, Chicago, Des Moines, and Atlantic City. The urban drawings immediately raise the question of the *architectural identity* of the American city. In every city a plurality of two- and three-dimensional configurations are interrelated in series of equivalencies such as streets/blocks, open spaces/buildings, object buildings/fabric, figural voids/fields, etc., as a multitude of floating signifiers.[28] What fixes their meaning is the quilting of the configurations by means of the architectural signifier — the gaze of the architect as opposed to the utilitarian gaze of the daily user, and to the gaze of the tourist looking for some presumed fixed identity. The urban drawings, in their transformations, iterations, and seriality, point to the impossibility of a definitive quilting and suggest instead a permanent process through which the American city is constantly reread and rewritten.[29]

The urban drawings not only expanded the repertory of analytical tools and strategies but also suggested the possible development of a specific American urbanism based on the formal conditions uncovered by the analysis. In 1989, I started working on the development of the Des Moines Vision Plan.[30] This process articulated the urban drawings — that is, the reading of the *specific formal armature* of the city with

24. Hubert Damisch and Jean Louis Cohen, *Americanisme et modernité* (Paris: Flammarion, 1993).

25. Mario Gandelsonas, *The Urban Text* (Cambridge, Mass.: The MIT Press, 1992).

26. Michel de Certeau, *The Practice of Everyday Life*, Steven Rendall, trans. (Berkeley: University of California Press, 1988).

27. Kevin Lynch, *The Image of the City* (Cambridge, Mass.: The MIT Press, 1960).

28. This presupposes an open, constantly shifting identity.

29. Slavoj Žižek, *The Sublime Object of Ideology* (London and New York: Verso, 1989).

30. See Diana Agrest and Mario Gandelsonas, *Works* (New York: Princeton Architectural Press, 1995).

31. Mario Gandelsonas, "The Master Plan as a Political Site," *Assemblage* 27 (Cambridge, Mass.: The MIT Press, 1996).

the local *sociopolitical and economic forces*. The entire process was based on different narratives in which we presented to the local community our readings of the basic formal moments in Des Moines in order to create a reaction, a dialogue, and an increasing awareness of the visual world in which the people of Des Moines live. This new articulation between the city and architecture that started with the dialogue generated by the urban drawings opened the planning processes to an architecture of the city and brought an additional political dimension to the urban drawings.[31]

**1**

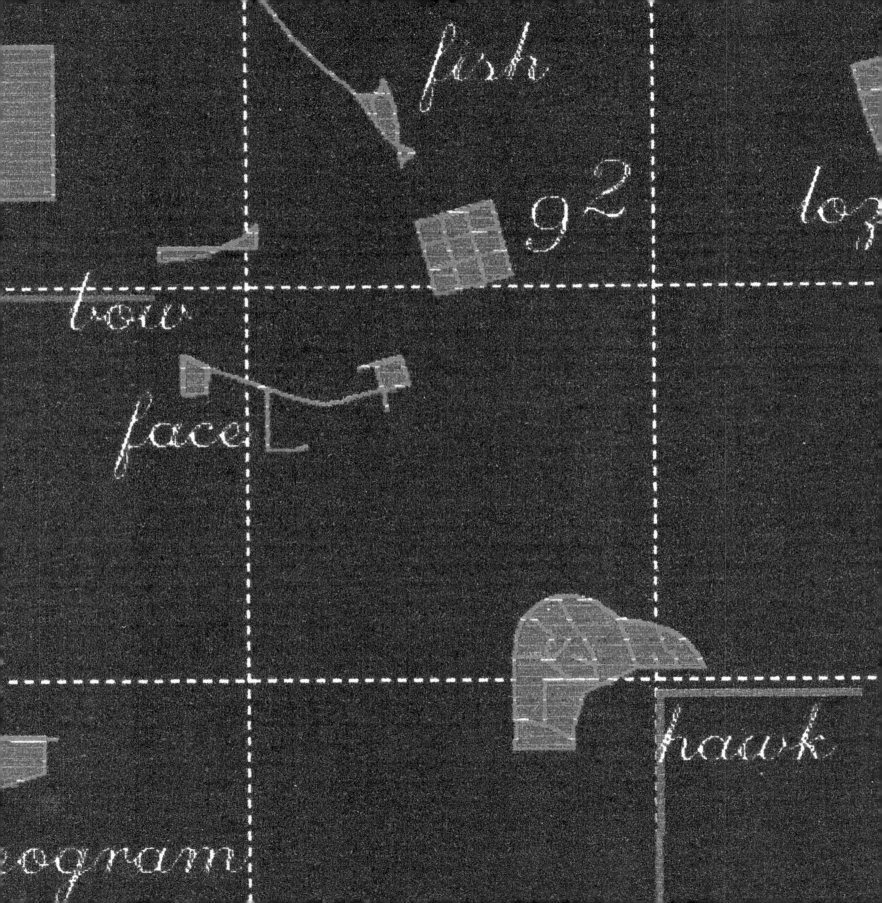

# The Western City: Seven Urban Scenes

**URBAN MUTATIONS: TRANSATLANTIC TRANSFERS AND EXCHANGES**

Two facts that played a significant role in structuring the American city took place only a few years apart but are rarely considered together. The first was the publication of Alberti's *Ten Books on Architecture* in 1485[1] and the second was the discovery of America in 1492. With Alberti's book, the European city became an unreachable object of desire for a new theory and practice of architecture: its plan, buildings, and spaces were fantasized as architectural configurations. With Columbus's discovery, Europe found the totality of which it formed a part.[2] America became the *other* space, fantasized both geographically as a "virgin" land and historically as a New World that would become "the scene of the future."

Why would a book that played a crucial role in establishing the practice of architecture as a liberal art in Europe influence the destiny of cities across the Atlantic Ocean? The answer is that the book set up a complex process involving architectural desire and urban identity that evolved along two trajectories. These trajectories converged in 1573 in the Law of Indies, where the architectural gridded plan was, for the first time, institutionalized as a basis for the foundation of the American city. The process of colonization of the New World opened up the possibility of founding new cities, thereby giving the urban scenarios described by Alberti —which could not be realized in the already-built cities of Europe — a "field" on which to project. America functioned as a screen where the colonizer attempted not just to recreate the European city, but also to inscribe imaginary architectural scenarios that had been "resisted" by the existing cities on the other side of the Atlantic.

As all constitutive acts do, Alberti's text structured and closed the practice it constitutes by establishing its identity. But it also produced a lack: the architectural apparatus that represents the building, the architectural atelier as the space where the practice takes place and the architect himself are separated and displaced from the construction process, its site, and the builder. The book filled the gap produced by the loss of the reality of the process of construction, and of the building itself, with a fantasy of an architectural universe of buildings. In this universe, the architectural city is seen as the largest possible building, and therefore the most ambitious fantasy. The architectural city, the one that starts from scratch and is configured according to the principles of the art, cannot be projected onto the existing European city that continues to grow by accretion and expansion. Columbus's discovery of America produced the place where this "architectural city" that starts from

1. Alberti, *The Ten Books of Architecture*. The book was presented to Nicolo V in 1452 and circulated until it was published in Florence in 1485.

2. Todorov, *La decouverte de l'amerique*.

scratch could be materialized. The New World offered the possibility for the architectural city to be implemented first through the Spanish codification of the Law of Indies and later through the influence of the other European colonial powers, France and England.

From the moment that the New World was discovered, the two edges of the Atlantic Ocean were part of a complex process of economic and cultural exchange where the flow of urban shapes and forms took place among different European and American cities. While during the first three hundred years the gridded plans and the Baroque diagonals came from Europe, in the nineteenth century the "American grids" were exported back,[3] followed by the skyscrapers of the early twentieth century when the American city became the model for cities all over the world. Modernist buildings were exported from Europe after the 1930s, and their architects followed just before World War II. The American freeway system moved to Europe in the 1960s and was followed by the office campus and X-Urban development. And this flow was more than a simple exchange: both sides of the Atlantic were also part of a circuit of desire where each side fantasized the other, where both Europe and America struggled to constitute their respective identities. Cities became the three-dimensional constructions that materialized these fantasies in different ways — America as the virgin land, as the setting for the scene of the future, and Europe as the already-built land that worked as a cultural repository, as the memory of the past.

I would like to describe the architecture of the American city as the result of the circulation and articulation of heterogeneous discourses, the *architectural* and the *urban*. I would also like to depict it as the projection of architectural fantasies of possible cities, as imaginary constructions first materialized in the form of discourses and drawings, and sometimes built when their intersection with urban processes happened at the right place and time (that is, when their articulation within the contingent urban processes brought them into reality).

The city constantly changes as a result of economic, political, and cultural forces. The change of the urban configurations that constantly develop and transform can be measured against a "datum" of permanent elements, the plan, the monuments. However, urban form not only transforms but also *mutates*.[4] In the long duration where the formal urban processes take place, there is a space of contingency where configurations are not derived from the existing shapes, but radically change. While urban transformations are measured in years, urban mutations, which occur in the long duration of history, are measured in centuries. They are determined mainly but not exclusively by economic and political forces. Their effects are vast and traumatic; they produce a major restructuring of existing conditions.

These formal mutations could be seen as the different *scenes* where the urban drama of the West has been *staged*. The play takes place in two radically different although interrelated scenes: the cities of the Old and the New World, in Europe and America, respectively.

3. See Camillo Sitte's critique of the American grids in *The Art of Building Cities* (New York: Reinhold Publishing, 1945).

4. The consideration of the architecture of the city determines the long historical view and avoids the "organic" metaphor underlying most transformational explanations, i.e., Kevin Lynch's explanation of the lineage of the contemporary city starting in the nineteenth century, where the great change involved the reconstruction of a substantial existing fabric of Paris and London. See Kevin Lynch, *Good City Form* (Cambridge, Mass.: The MIT Press, 1987). Via Giulia in Rome contradicts this view and its importance can only be understood in a history of the articulation between "architecture" and the city.

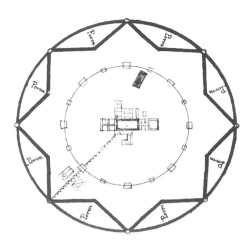

I have structured the scenes in two different ways — one spatially, the other one along the temporal axis. They are played by different actors, architectural and nonarchitectural. These actors are engaged in actions that can be seen as choreographed by forces of desire pointed at different unattainable objects. The scenes are viewed by different observers, including the actors themselves.

I will present a series of synchronic sections where schematic depictions of the actors and actions take place in six different scenes, and a possible scenario for the seventh scene that is being written right now. The first and the fifth scene take place in the Imaginary dimension within the practice of Architecture, while the others take place in the reality of the city. Scenes one, two, and five take place in Europe, and architectural actors and actions command the stage. In scenes three, four, six, and X, the X-Urban scene (which take place in America), the city dominates the foreground. The last two scenes, 6 and X, represent a break with respect to all the previous cities, a break more profound than the apparent break proposed in scene 5, by the city of modernist urbanism. Although these scenes are presented chronologically, their construction should be seen as the retroactive effect of the latest X-Urban scene where the author resides.

## SCENE 1
# The Renaissance City

### THE CITY INHABITS ARCHITECTURE

The first radical change to affect the configuration of the Western city takes place in the architectural Imaginary where a mutation with respect to the medieval city is staged. The starting point of our story is located in the discursive realm of the Renaissance theories of architecture. A fantasy that will return in a number of architectural theories, it is first displayed in Alberti's treatise *The Ten Books of Architecture*.[5] In Book 4, on public works, Alberti proposes that "thorough consideration should be given to the city's layout, site, and outline." The urban fantasy appears in the form of the centralized plans of what was going to become the ideal Renaissance city.[6] The geometric configuration of the outline of the new city was to be a "circle, rectangle, or whatever shape,"when located on a level and open plain.[7] The city and its different urban moments are articulated into structured pairs of oppositions. These oppositions organize the architectural and the urban signifiers, stabilizing their meanings: the wall of the city versus the ditch, the gates versus the major axes, the streets (straight versus curved) versus the public squares, the sacred buildings versus the secular buildings and the public buildings versus the private buildings.

This fantasy presents a stark contrast to the reality of the contemporary medieval city that grows "as a stain of oil," as Giulio Carlo Argan points out in the case of Rome,[8] which until the 1400s develops "around the medieval nucleus of the 'piazza del ponte'" (located across the Castel Sant'angelo). This growth is produced by the aggregation of

5. Alberti, *The Ten Books of Architecture*. Alberti's treatise is described by Argan as the first treatise on urbanism. "It is the founding treatise of urbanism as discipline, and that is precisely where it differs from Vitruvius's treatise.... The city provides both the idea that supports the notion of building and the dimension in which the activity of architecture is inscribed." Giulio Carlo Argan, "The treatise de re Aedificatoria" in *Storia dell'arte come storia della cité* (Ed. Riunitti, 1983).

6. Alberti, *The Ten Books of Architecture*. As Argan says in his book Art and the City, Alberti is more interested in the genesis of the city that in its final form. While the question of configuration in mentioned in a few sentences, and layout is described without any formal precision, he elaborates at length on the question of site. However, the principles proposed in his book are going to inform most architectural urban fantasies developed in the sixteenth century.

7. Ibid.

8. Giulio Carlo Argan, *El Concepto del espacio Arquitectonico* (Buenos Aires: Nueva Vision, 1966).

INSET: Via Giulia and Via Lungara as shown
in the Nolli plan

RIGHT: Via Giulia, view from Farnese Palace

buildings and of small neighborhoods without any plans. Alberti's architectural fantasy proposes a radical critique of this city: the planning of the city as a totality with geometric configurations. The city is depicted as a unified entity that presupposes a totalizing apprehension. It is metaphorically described as a building, it is portrayed in similar terms as a physical body composed of parts: actual buildings, public spaces, monuments, public/private buildings, and so on. This reflects a conception of the physical world seen as structured in different levels, where similar rules apply at every level. A city (a large "house") is equivalent to a house (a small "city"). The city is made out of buildings, in the same way in which buildings are made out of rooms, or elements of buildings.[9] The defensive wall of the city reifies it and provides its objecthood. The wall could be a solid or a void (i.e., a ditch), it could be physical or nonphysical (when military prowess of its citizens function as the wall of the city[10]).

The city is a building to be seen but also a viewing mechanism, a scopic device that is ideally located in the middle of its territory with buildings that will be reified by the designs of ideal cities. The Renaissance architectural fantasy obscures the fact that the city occurs in the temporal dimension, that it is a process and not an object, and that, if there is always a possibility of a synchronic cut in this process, the configuration of this object is given by its voids and not by its solids, by its streets and squares rather than by its buildings. An organic metaphor allows us to fantasize the origin of the city, the city in embryo, the

military camp, that could be rectangular or circular in plan.[11] In the gridded plan, the preferred configuration, the "military streets" links the gates. The fantasy of the city as building suppresses the differences between building and city, devalues the formal potential of the voids, and obscures the indeterminate and temporal nature of the urban processes.

## ARCHITECTURE INHABITS THE CITY

The realization of the architectural urban fantasy takes place in two different stages: the already-built city in Europe and the "virgin" land in America. It is played by two different actors: architects in Europe and by nonarchitects in America.

In Europe, the fantasy of the architectural city is fully realized in paintings and theatrical stagesets,[12] through its ideological articulation with the painterly and scenographic practices of its time.[13] However, its implementation in the European city is limited and fragmentary. One of the earliest attempts takes place in Rome with Donato Bramante's urban plan for Pope Julius II and Pope Leo X. An architectural geometry is projected onto the city of Rome and materialized into streets that cut through the existing medieval fabric. The first implementation of the architectural city takes place with the piercing of Via Giulia and Via Lungara, a street parallel to the first on the other side of the Tiber River.[14] Via Giulia stands as one of the first attempts to inscribe this imaginary city in the context of the existing European city. This medieval city is not about form but about density, about how close

9. Alberti, *The Ten Books of Architecture*, 23.

10. Ibid., 101–3.

11. Ibid., 131–3.

12. This articulation between urban fantasy and artistic practices will be constantly restructured through history and is being restructured today.

13. Hubert Damisch, *The Origin of Perspective* (Cambridge, Mass.: The MIT Press, 1995).

14. Arnaldo Buschi, *Bramante* (London and New York: Thames and Hudson, 1973), 124. See also Luigi Salerno, Luigi Spezzaferro, and Manfredo Tafuri, *Via Giulia* (Rome: Casa Editrice Stabilimento, 1973).

together or scattered the buildings were.[15] Density given by contiguity is the basic pragmatic principle of a city politically organized around a center or centers of baronial power.

Bramante's plan intends to establish a more fluid communication between various parts of the tightly knit medieval city by breaking up the baronial social fabric. But this operation does not produce an urban transformation: the plan is only partially carried out, due to the resistance that the formless town presented to the radical changes embodied in the architectural urban fantasy.

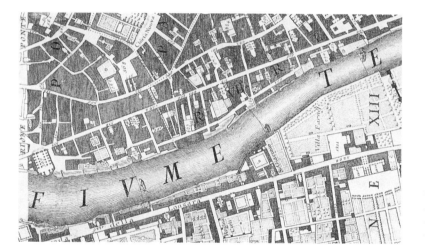

America offers the land where the architectural Renaissance city could be inscribed and implemented, particularly through the regulations for the foundation of new cities imposed by the Spanish Law of Indies of 1573.[16] The Spanish colonization of the New World began more than a century before the other European countries' successful efforts.[17] An arc from the Gulf states to New Mexico and up through California to the Golden Gate delimits the land formerly subject to Spanish rule.[18] The first of these Spanish cities in what would become U.S. territory is St. Augustine, Florida, founded in 1587. The last one, Los Angeles, founded almost two hundred years later, is the city where the first colonial grid, the original pueblo grid, meets the post-Revolutionary continental grid that provided the armature of the contemporary megacity.

The Spanish settlements were the first to establish the *grid* as the principle for the urban organization of the American city. While the English colonization continues the same pattern, their urban plans become a site for urban experimentation. The town of New Haven, Connecticut, founded in 1638, is in its minimal simplicity a paradigmatic example of a new *scale* in the configuration of the gridded plan: a very large nine-square grid (825 square feet total) with a central green destined to become the geometric core of the city. The diagonal streets that continue the orthogonal streets outwards to provide access to the fields surrounding the town become the city's armature as a chaotic background that accentuates the clarity of the core.

15. Fernand Braudel, *The Identity of France* (New York: Harper & Row, 1989), 130–1.

16. The Law of Indies, which was already at work as early as 1561, determined the planning of hundreds of towns and cities. See Reps, *The Making of Urban America*, 29; and Urbanism Español en America (Madrid: Editora Nacional, 1973).

17. The first successful settlement in the New World was Santo Domingo established in 1496, although it was moved to another site in 1501.

18. Reps, *The Making of Urban America*, 26.

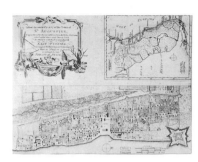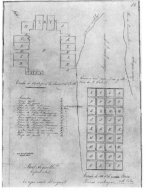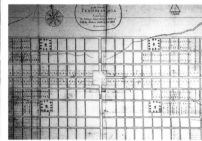

William Penn's 1682 plan of Philadelphia, the first large American city to be laid out on a gridded plan, is also organized around a central square where the two main streets intersect. However, a figure created by a second ring of four residential squares establishes a similarity with a configuration that had often structured the architectural fantasies of ideal cities. Reps suggests a number of possible sources for this plan, in particular one of the projects for the rebuilding of London after the Great Fire of 1666. While the plan of Christopher Wren is the one associated to that event, a lesser-known plan by Richard Newcourt bears an uncanny formal resemblance to Penn's plan, with a similar arrangement of a central square and four residential squares. The plan of Philadelphia was to have an important role as a model for many towns created in the westward march of urbanization.

In the 1735 plan of Savannah, Georgia, the multiplication of squares transforms the role of open public spaces from figure to texture. The origin of the plan might be traced to Georgian London where in the late seventeenth century and early eighteenth century a number of squares were built in proximity of each other.[19] In the American version a rich variety of public spaces is posited in the new plan for the city, as opposed to the carving of the existing fabric in the English version. The plan of Savannah presents a complex texture of solids and voids articulated by a syntactic counterpoint. The very large wards — similar in size to the New Haven blocks — present a very sophisticated internal configuration where a system of oppositions establishes differ-ences between solids and voids; private buildings (on 60' x 90' lots) and public buildings (on trustee lots fronting the square); main streets (75' wide) and secondary streets (37.5' wide), and streets and service lanes (22.5' wide).[20]

The American city will become the *other* of Europe, the imaginary city that cannot be built in Europe, or only built in a fragmentary way in the already-built territory of the European city. The built city in Europe and the absence of architecture in America — architecture is only an "influence" in the plan — confirm very early on the impossbility of the *architectural city*, of bringing together architecture and the city.

19. Reps refers specifically to Red Lion Square (1684),
St. James Square (1684), Grosvenor Square (1695),
Hanover Square (1712), and Cavendish Square (1720).
Reps, *The Making of the American City*, 199.

20. James Bailey, ed., *New Towns in America*
(New York: John Wiley & Sons, 1970).

LEFT: St. Augustine, Florida, 1556, early foundation plan, c. 1770; Plan of Los Angeles, 1781; Plan of New Haven, Connecticut, 1748; Plan of Philadelphia, 1682

LEFT INSET: View of Savannah, Georgia, 1740

BELOW: Plan of Rome, new streets linking the monuments

## SCENE 2
# The Baroque City

The second mutation of urban form also takes place within the realm of architecture. However, instead of developing a fantasy in a discourse detached from urban reality, this mutation takes the city as a point of departure.

The staging of this new city occurs in the last twenty years of the sixteenth century when the Pope Sixtus V and the architect Domenico Fontana produce an urban project for Rome by connecting major churches. Instead of conceptualizing the city as a system of solids, Fontana's proposal presents Rome as a network of voids to be overlapped onto the existing city. While the Rome of the 1500s contained *sacred monuments* — in particular Saint Peter's but also other churches — the new Rome becomes a *sacred city* that is conceived for liturgical circulation. At the same time, this circuit functions as a tourist attraction and therefore as an element of the commercial network.[21] The carving operation is similar to the one that materialized in a very limited way through Via Giulia. The new network of diagonal streets and boulevards (that is, of voids) is pierced through the same fabric where the first attempts to inscribe the geometry of the Renaissance city took place. However, the Baroque city represents a radical change with respect to the ideal Renaissance city, in terms of the articulation of the architectural discourse with the physical city. The Baroque city, which is contingent to the location of monuments, is directly inscribed onto the physical city rather than described by the discourse of architecture. An important second attempt to realize this new city, one that will

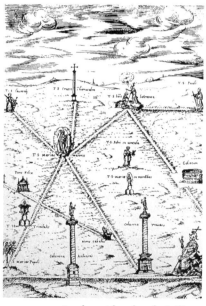

become the dominant form of urban restructuring in Europe until the end of the nineteenth century, takes place in France, in the design of a fantastic city outside the city: the garden of Versailles.[22] André Le Nôtre starts the planing of Versailles in 1662 and continues working on the project until his death in 1700. The notion of axis cutting through fabric had already been implemented in Paris with the royal axis. However, the desire of a totalizing design is not fully developed until Versailles. The specificity of Versailles is given by the territorial scale of its composition: the previous gardens are conceived as islands of civilization and pleasure in the middle of a chaotic territory perceived as hostile. The garden layers three different scales: the 93 hectares of gardens, the 700 hectares of the "Petit Parc," and, finally, the 6,500 hectares of the "Grand Parc" that visually erase the 43 kilometers of wall that enclose it.[23] Le Nôtre's radical transformation can also be seen as an

21. Argan, *El Concepto del espacio Arquitectonico*.

22. Sigfried Giedion proposes that Baroque Rome first travels to France, and materializes in Versailles when the Popes move to Avignon. Sigfried Giedion, *Space, Time, and Architecture* (Cambridge, Mass.: Harvard University Press, 1982).

23. Pierre Andre Lablande, *Les Jardins de Versailles* (Paris: Editions Scala, 1995).

experiment that examines and realizes the piercing faculty of the gaze, in this case the royal gaze: all the views converge to the royal eye. Le Nôtre's plan deploys a systematic investigation of different formal devices that frame, refract, or stop the gaze, that literally blur its object through the colossal military scale of the perspective views, providing the perceptual experience of the Baroque notion of infinite.

In the second half of the nineteenth century, the articulation of an authoritarian urbanism and the new structures of capitalism produce the restructuring of the major European capitals accomplished through the application of some of the basic principles of the Baroque city. In Berlin, Barcelona, St. Petersburg, Budapest, Vienna, and particularly in Paris, the inscription of a new city is literally overlapped onto the historic city, with axes that cut through the medieval fabric, deadending in monuments.

The Hausmannian restructuring of Paris, along with Vienna's Ringstrasse, could be seen as the culmination of the urban experiments partially accomplished in Rome and fully developed as a totalizing landscape in Le Nôtre's plan for Versailles. The notion of the city conceived as a *network* that organizes movement was already established when Baron Georges-Eugène Haussmann comes to the Perfecture de Paris in June 1853. However, the major restructuring takes place when he conceives and implements the second and most extensive network, which was proposed and approved in 1858. A third restructuring was begun in 1868. The Haussmannian operation projects a mechanicist

ideology in the name of hygiene and social order, as a way to prevent disease (cholera) and social uprising (revolution). The straight lines that pierce, widen, and align the new or existing streets through the diseased physical and social fabric condense beauty, hygiene, and commerce. In its totalizing scope, the urban operation blurs the classical opposition between spontaneous versus planned cities or new cities (which was the term used to designate the colonial cities in virgin territories; i.e., the American city), proposing a third term, the restructured city.[24] While the city was defined in Diderot and d'Alembert's 1757 *Encyclopédie ou Dictionnaire raisonné des sciences, des arts et des métiers* as a finite and ordered group of buildings, in the Haussmannian city, the place assigned to circulation, the new network of streets and boulevards, rule the buildings.[25]

Vienna's Ringstrasse is contemporary of Hausmannian Paris. However, despite that the scale and grandeur suggest the persistent power of the Baroque, the conditions and the configuration in Vienna are the opposite of Paris. The construction of the Ringstrasse as a vast complex of public buildings and private dwellings occupied the ring of open land separating the inner city from its suburbs. "The Baroque planners had organized space to carry the viewer to a central focus: space served as a setting to the buildings that dominated it.... The Ringstrasse inverts the Baroque procedure, using the unrelated buildings to magnify the horizontal space,"[26] a space that preannounces the modernist field. As opposed to the *radial* configuration of Versailles,

24. However, the restructured city will be immediately caught into another opposition that defines two opposed strategies in dealing with the spontaneous city: demolition (Haussmann) versus restauration (Violet-Le-Duc).

25. Marcel Roncayolo, "La production de la ville" in Jean de Cars and Pierre Pinon, *Haussman* (Paris: Ed du pavillion de l'arsenal, 1991). This urban restructuring took also place in provincial cities such as Lyon, Marseilles, Lille, and Bordeaux, and also in smaller towns such as Avignon and Montpellier.

26. Carl E. Schorske, *Fin-de-Siecle Vienna: Politics and Culture* (New York: Alfred A. Knopf, 1980).

FAR LEFT: Versailles, view of the chateau and the garden; Rue de Rivoli, Paris, aerial view

LEFT: Vienna, plan

INSET: Albrecht Dürer, *Drawing of Reclining Woman*; camera obscura

RIGHT: St. Peter's Square, aerial view

which influenced the Haussmannian conception of a multicentered network, the Ringstrasse proposes a *concentric* configuration. "The plan suppressed the vistas in favor of a circular flow without architectonic containment, and without visible destination."[27] The competition in 1858 marks the starting point and the construction of the Ringstrasse takes place over the next thirty years.

## ARCHITECTURE INHABITS THE CITY

While the restructuring of the city is drastic, the restructuring of the subject is equally radical. The mutation that produces the Baroque city is overdetermined by the passage from the observer of perspective to the observer of the camera obscura.[28] There are the obvious differences affecting the two observers: the interiorized observer of an exterior world is separated from that world in the case of the camera obscura; as opposed to the observer of perspective, a procedure of picture-making by means of the construction of a two-dimensional representation of the exterior world where image and object belong to the same indistinct reality. In the camera obscura, the relationship is established between apparatus and reality, and the nondistinction between reality and its pro-

jection is abolished. As Jonathan Crary says, perhaps one of the most impressive features of the camera obscura was the representation of movement that had been suppressed in perspective.[29] One of the radical differences between the Renaissance subject of perspective, fixated in space, and the subject of the camera obscura is mobility, not only of the image, but also of the subject, who observes a projection independent from his fixed position. Another implication of the division between interiorized subject and exteriorized world is that this "exterior" world can be shaped, and as such it is a potential object of architecture.

In fact this exterior world in the context of the city, what we could today call urban space, constitutes the object of architecture in a number of major Baroque projects of which St. Peter's Square is a preeminent example. According to Argan, Gian Lorenzo Bernini's design implied a mobile observer that correlated the plan of the square to the dominant configurations offered by the building. The square is conceived as two moments. In the first moment, the observer relates the two half-circles of the plan to a dome that gradually diminishes visually to give place to the facade. In the second moment, when the observer enters the antiperspectival room, which visually "slows down" the movement, the facade becomes the dominant feature, the wall that separates the exterior from the interior. The building becomes simply a mediating structure between urban voids and interior voids.

The site for the practice of architecture in the Baroque city expands beyond the building to include the design of figural urban rooms (such

27. Ibid.

28. Jonathan Crary, *Techniques of the Observer* (Cambridge, Mass.: The MIT Press, 1990).

29. Ibid., 34.

BELOW: L'Enfant's plan for Washington, D.C., aerial view

RIGHT: Burnham's plan of Chicago

FAR RIGHT CLOCKWISE FROM TOP LEFT: Plot of 36 sections,
Land Ordinance of 1785; Plan of Missouri City, Missouri, 1836;
one-mile-grid, aerial view

as the Place Royales in Paris and in London) and street facades as urban scenography (such as the Rue de Rivoli in Paris and the Crescents in London). While America provides the stage where the Renaissance architectural fantasies will be "materialized," the reality of the BaroqueEuropean city provides the "material" for an American urban fantasy. This model travels to America and materializes in the plan of Washington, D.C. The design of the city that represents the

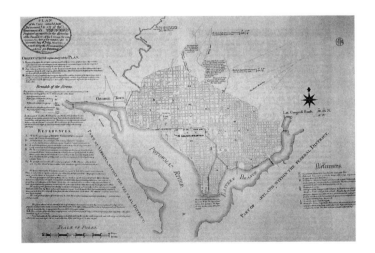

union of all the states takes place in a sequence of traumatic events closely related to Europe. The drama develops in two acts, the first of which is the foundation of Washington, D.C., and the second of which is the completion of the plan of the Mall. The former drama is acted by a European architect in America, Pierre Charles L'Enfant; the latter takes place in Europe where the monumental axis is designed in a charrette while American architects visit a number of European cities. In L'Enfant's plan for Washington, the Baroque city is overlapped onto the grid, in contrast to Thomas Jefferson's proposal based on a gridded plan. Washington is the American city that *condensates* European and architectural desires; it stands for the European city with an American scale and grid.[30] Once established, Washington will represent the "other" American city, the formally overregulated city, where the sectional freedom of its buildings is suppressed.

The fully developed version of the Baroque city, Paris, travels to America at the beginning of the twentieth century with Burnham's plan for Chicago.[31] The City Beautiful movement, as an ideology, will be in the end only partially implemented: the political differences between the European and American contexts, particularly the weak role of government in American democracy, will stand as an obstacle to its development.

30. The original plan for Washington, D.C., was vast, measuring 5,700 acres.

31. Daniel H. Burnham, Edward H. Bennett, and Charles Moore, eds., *Plan of Chicago* (reprint, New York: Princeton Architectural Press, 1993).

## SCENE 3

# The Continental Grid
# and the
# Gridded American City

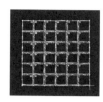
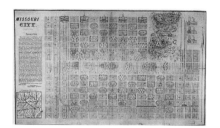

In scenes 3 and 4, the action moves to North America where new mutations of urban form take place at the end of both the eighteenth and nineteenth centuries. Only 140 years after the Mayflower arrives at Cape Cod in 1620, one million English people are densely settled in the three major northeastern cities: Boston, New York, and Philadelphia. These cities, grown out of the wilderness, exist in a state of semifreedom similar to that of the typical cities of Europe in the Middle Ages.[32] "The very young America of 1776 is geographically reduced to the Atlantic. It is economically an agricultural country, socially dominated by landowners."[33]

The break in the colonial link with England opens the road to the construction of the first democracy of the modern times. It also opens up the potential for a new chapter in the formal development of the Western city and the establishment of new urban experiments. America will not be just a "scene of the future" where Europe will project its fantasies,[34] but also an urban laboratory for those who wanted to build a new society.[35]

The continental one-mile grid, which marks the appropriation of the land by this new society, resulted from the inscription of the Second Continental Congress's Land Ordinance of 1785, an early mapping of the territory of America. The urban implications of this colossal grid are present in its association with the definition of "township." The origin of the U.S. land survey system has been associated with Thomas Jefferson, who chaired a committee in 1784 to prepare a plan for

the government of the Western Territory. His proposal divided the land into square miles oriented along the four cardinal points.[36] The Land Ordinance provided for the sale of western lands by laying out six-square-mile townships, each divided into thirty-six sections of one square mile.[37] The survey of the first seven ranges completed in 1786 was based on this one-square-mile grid. The marking of the American territory can

32. Braudel, *The History of Civilizations*.

33. Ibid.

34. Damisch and Cohen, *Americanisme et modernite*.

35. The order — political, economic, ideological — created by the Founding Fathers (who "had the will and the certitude to create the best constitution of the world imposed by the under the names of liberty and equality") is already the order of capitalism. (Braudel, *A History of Civilizations*, 508.) Braudel discusses competition in America as more fair than in European capitalism. While in Europe the benefits are reserved for a very small and closed class, in the more open American society, everyone has the chance — at least in theory — of making it: this is the place of the self-made man.

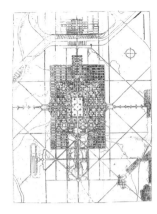

LEFT: Le Corbusier's Ville Contemporaine

RIGHT: William Le Baron Jenney, Monadnock Building, Chicago

FAR RIGHT: The skyscraper: a diagram showing formal transformation and circulation of meanings in the evolution of the type

be seen as the "anticipated inversion" of an operation of measurement that will take place in Europe a few years later, between 1792 and 1799. While in Europe the measurement of the meridianal arc between two European cities, Dunkirk and Barcelona, provide the basis for the definition of the official meter,[39] in America a colossal unit of measurement, the mile, is taken as a base for a mutated territorial urban grid that became the trace of the largest continental megalopolis at the end of the twentieth century.

The urban implications of the gridding of America do not develop until the mid-nineteenth century because the focus in the young republic is on the sea and not on the land.[39] In the 1850s, with the competition of the English "steamers," an enormous new project starts displacing America's focus from the sea to the continent: the conquest of the West and the building of the railroads, the internal navigation lines.[40] In the nineteenth century, the colossal grid — extended as a cartographic and economic political device to map the territory of the Union and to stimulate land speculation — becomes the formal ground for the displacement of the frontier as a material and spiritual adventure. It was also the basis for the planning of most cities west of the Appalachians extending all the way to the West Coast. This rural grid will become urban when the single line of the geometric grid will be doubled to become a road, when the line as boundary or property line is transformed into the double line of a space of circulation, as in the cases of Chicago, Des Moines, Los Angeles, and many other cities.

The continental grid belongs to the same regime of visuality as the Baroque city, as the materialization of questions raised in Europe by the camera obscura and answered in the New World. The camera obscura as seen by Descartes is a mechanism that allows the orderly and calculable penetration of light rays through a single opening that corresponds to the flooding of the mind by the light of reason."[41] This mechanism corresponds to the cartesian space where all objects of thought, regardless of subject matter, can be ordered and compared. This Cartesian space reverberates with the gridded American territory that becomes the ground, the *field of projection*, where the play of geographical and historical differences represented by the Union takes place.

Why call the one-mile grid an urban mutation? Because it produces a number of displacements, first in size and scale; second in the planar as opposed to the punctual centralized city of the classical treatises; and third in the way space is subordinated to time in a city without "walls" of infinite possible extension, the city of movement where one circulates rather than the city of object-buildings where one lives or works. The American grid presupposes continuous fluid movement, as opposed to the static "urban rooms" of the Renaissance perspective, a movement that had been suppressed in perspective and therefore in the Renaissance city, but also movement in a space without boundaries as opposed to the restructured Baroque city.

Articulated to the one-mile grid, an extended exploration of the gridded plan takes place. New gridded cities are created as multiple

36. Hildegard Binder Johnson, "Towards a National Landscape," in Michael P. Conzen, ed., *The Making of the American Landscape* (London: Unwin Hyman, 1990), 127.

37. Reps, *The Making of Urban America*.

38. Patrick Bouchareine, "Le metre, la seconde et la vitesse de la lumiere" in *La Recherche* 91 (1978), mentioned by Paul Virilio in *The Lost Dimension* (New York: Semiotext(e), 1991).

39. At the end of the eighteenth century the American fleet surpasses all the other nations with the exception of England. See Braudel, *A History of Civilizations*, 505.

40. Ibid., 507.

41. Crary, *Techniques of the Observer*, 42.

translations, transformations, and mutations in an endless process of rewriting.[42] This is a new American gridded plan that presupposes both a boundless field where it is inscribed and a different syntax.[43] However, the notion of the field remains invisible until the twentieth century, when it acquires a prominent role with the modernist movement. Modernist urbanism will reveal the field as an urban notion that was not always explicit, but always implied by the American city.

## THE CITY INHABITS ARCHITECTURE

For the American continental grid to inhabit architecture we have to wait until it is introduced in Europe by modernist urbanism when Le Corbusier, in a double movement, gentrifies the colossal surveyors grid, transforming it into the architectural grid of 400 meters by 400 meters that defines the urban field of Ville Contemporaine. At the same time, this grid suppresses the infinite variation and contingencies of the speculative gridded American city with the fantasy of a geometric grid that supposedly defines the plan of the American city. In a sense, while proposing the straight line and street in opposition to Camillo Sitte, Le Corbusier aligns himself with Sitte's view of America as the place where the *neutral* grid reigns.

# The City of Skyscrapers

While all the previous cities are determined by their plan, in America a new city is built at the end of the nineteenth and beginning of the twentieth century, a city where the section becomes independent of the plan, the city of skyscrapers.

This urban mutation takes place through the invention of a new urban type, the skyscraper, made possible by the development of steel structures and by Elisha Graves Otis's invention of the technology of the elevator. The difference in the development of this type between America and Europe is the difference between the architect's ideology and the ideology of the engineer. In Europe, for instance, Alexandre-Gustave Eiffel's conception of the configuration of the skyscraper is not subject to the architectural discourse. It relates to the bridge rather than the building (the Eiffel tower is a vertical bridge) or to the colossal (the statue of Liberty is a figural skyscraper).

Whereas the first-generation skyscrapers in Chicago are extrusions of the plan, the New York skyscrapers are defined by a section. When the "ascending line of force of an organism of potentially infinite development is given free reign", as in New York City, this new type becomes an "anarchic individual"[44] that antagonizes the city. The skyscraper exacerbates a latent typological characteristic of the American city: the tendency for buildings to "behave" as independent and *scattered* objects and not as part of a "collective" fabric of *attached* buildings, as in the case of the European city. The skyscraper embodies this condition as a building-object, as an urban building that both depends on and ignores

42. These grids were different from the earlier Spanish grids because they are articulated to the colossal one-mile grid. This grid separates itself from architecture in that it is not marked with centers or borders, although it is not an abstract geometric grid either. We will come back to these issues in the second chapter.

43. An example of this different syntax can be found in another one of Jefferson's inventions: the checkerboard plan. Two alternative readings of the checkerboard pattern are possible: first, a garden with fabric placed on top in a checkered pattern or, second, a city carved with gardens in checkerboard pattern. This first reveals the closure of the opposition and each side presupposes the other. Also, the

pattern allows the reading of the field where both readings can be seen as an operation based on either addition or subtraction.

44. Manfredo Tafuri, "The Disenchanted Mountain: The Skyscraper and the City," in Ciucci, et al., *The American City*, 389–90.

RIGHT: Jan Purkinje, *Afterimages*, 1823

FAR RIGHT: Empire State Building, New York City

the city, as "a building that remains aloof of the city."[45] The architectural implication of this new typological conception is a city where the section becomes independent of the plan.

In the American city, the attached fabric is a historical glitch, the result of the economic constraints that force the buildings to be contiguous in high-density situations. The objecthood of buildings is maintained in sections where they are free to compete with each other and ignore their neighbor, in contrast with the European cities where the public cornices rules the individual buildings. As Manieri Elia remarks when describing the urban architecture of the American city, "the urban character... was... conditioned by the rigid, two-dimensional nature of the ordinary grid of streets; thus the margin of volumetric liberty... consisted exclusively in the third dimension ... apart from the rare cases ... this third dimension had no organic proportional relationship to the other two."[46] In other words, the American city stands for the failure of architecture in the city. It is this fact that allows for an examination of the plan independently of the buildings sitting upon it; it is also this fact that makes it difficult to work analytically with the notion of urban types in the context of the American city. In fact, the skyscraper itself escapes the notion of type that has been critically reformulated to deal with the transformational behavior of typologies in the American context.[47] In the American city, the buildings play their own game with different degrees of autonomy within the constraints of the gridded plan. In the case of the skyscraper, where the question of height is crucial, the determinations are

economic. The steel-frame skyscraper is the perfect physical embodiment of the dense and heavily centralized city.[48] The Chicago Loop is the perfect product of this laissez-faire city: "a regular grid in high density situations and an assemblage of prismatic buildings, the height of which is determined by the investment of capital."[49]

The skyscraper completes the process initiated by Goethe when he closes the hole of the camera obscura, producing a new "psychological" space of vision[50] and signaling the end of the classical observer. The afterimage created by this closing opens up a new period of scopic inventions, and also a new observer who is defined by the nineteenth-century theories concerning its physiology and psychology. This is the same ambulatory observer, subject to the new and complex stimulation provided by the European city, as described by Walter Benjamin as "an observer shaped by a convergence of new urban spaces, technologies and new economic and symbolic functions of images and products — forms of artificial lighting, new use of mirrors, glass and steel architecture, railroads, museums, gardens, photography, fashion crowds. Perception is temporal and kinetic ... there is never a pure access to a single object; vision is always multiple, adjacent to and overlapping with other objects, desires, and vectors."[51] The American city exposed this observer to the same type of stimuli but framed by a new city, by the savage energy of the skyscraper, a first attempt to articulate the machine and urban architecture that broke away with the classical city. The imperatives of capitalist modernization simultaneously demolish

45. Ibid., 389.

46. This is a way for Manieri Elia to indicate the lack of an architectural relation. Manieri Elia, "Toward an Imperial City," in Ciucci, et al., *The American City*.

47. See Agrest, *Architecture from Without*.

48. The elevator, the telephone, and the electric bulb made life in the tall buildings possible and bearable. The skyscraper established a systematic relation with the streetcar, which, unlike the railroads, penetrated the very heart of the city; its tracks radiated from the center where the department stores where located.

49. Elia, "Toward an Imperial City," in Ciucci, et al., *The American City*.

50. Crary, *Techniques of the Observer*, 68.

51. Ibid., 20.

the field of classical vision and the classical city itself: *the skyscraper represents the end of the conception of the classical city of fabric.*

The skyscraper is the visible urban building (as opposed to the visible architectural monument) and the viewing building (so named because it looks at the city), embodying the dialectics of seeing and being seen.[52] In Europe, this condition is symbolized by the Eiffel Tower, which was a solitary skyscraper in a city of fabric. In America, the skyscraper represents the paradox of a building that tries to visually capture the city at the point where it extends beyond the limits of vision, at the time when the centralized city starts its decline and the germ of a new suburban city starts to develop. The urban structure of the skyscraper city involves not just the central business district surrounded with factories and poor neighborhoods, but also the large outer ring of middle-class suburbs and the country retreats of the very rich. This emerging suburban city is served by roads that condense green space and movement, the parkways,[53] which could be seen as the displaced parks that could not be built inside the city of skyscrapers.[54] By the turn of the century this "new city" was fully constituted, supplementing the skyscraper "walking city"; it will become three times larger that the older "walking city." Segregated by class (reserved for the middle class) and function (habitation), the new city was destined to supplant the old and become the preeminent American urban form.

52. Roland Barthes, *La Tour Eiffel* (Paris: Delpire, 1964).

53. The most important network of parkways was built in New York, the paradigmatic city of skyscrapers, by Robert Moses in the 1930s.

54. Building parks would be a contradiction in terms with a city based on increasing density (they would diminish the density).

LEFT: Le Corbusier's Ville Contemporaine

RIGHT INSET: Le Corbusier's Collage for Plan Voisin

## ARCHITECTURE INHABITS THE CITY

What is the role of architecture in the city of skyscrapers? The design of the skyscraper opens up the question of an American architecture and therefore the question of its identity, of America's relationship with the other, with Europe. There is also the question of architecture itself, which resides in Europe, and this very difficult question will bring architecture into crisis: the new situation is very different from the first two European mutations in the way that architecture inhabits the city. It is not an architecture that is sure of itself and of its principles but an architecture in crisis that faces the city through the traumatic experience of forming a new urban type that resists the architectural European tradition. "The architects of the Chicago school, who, in their heyday created the first skyscrapers, famous for their undeniably high quality and fascination, were dedicated to originality. Although their work may have been constrained by an inevitable inferiority complex with respect to Europe, their objective was the foundation of a uniquely American architecture, one whose debt to Europe would be no more than that of any innovative architecture to tradition."[55]

## THE CITY INHABITS ARCHITECTURE

The official program for the Chicago Tribune competition was wholly concerned with "formal eloquence," that is, with architecture. Thus, Tafuri is provided an ideal context in which to examine the relations between European and American architectural cultures, and we are provided the opportunity to examine the impossible articulation of the modern city of skyscrapers and architecture. Modernist urbanism, the architectural urban fantasy developed at the beginning of the twentieth century, is still the dominant architectural urban model. It relates to the first city, the Renaissance city, insofar as it takes place primarily in the discursive realm and in the imaginary dimension. It is proposed as a radical critique of the existing city of fabric. Le Corbusier, a central figure of modernism, realizes in the early teens that the practice of architecture as it had existed was no longer possible. The sources of the problematization of the practice are related to the relentless industrialization of production and the new division of labor, but also to the new means of architectural production (new construction technologies) and reproduction (the media). Confronting this crisis, Le Corbusier will propose three deaths: first, to "kill" classical architecture in order to assure the survival of *Architecture*, an architecture that resonates with the new spirit of the times; second, to "kill" the classical city of fabric and replace it with a modernist city of objects; and finally, to "kill" contemporary urbanism (that is, the urbanism of Camillo Sitte), which looks at the past as a model and therefore contradicts the new spirit. In the end, Le Corbusier wants to guarantee the architectural control of urbanism and of the city, an insistent theme throughout the history of architecture. In *Precisions on the State of Architecture and Urbanism*, Le Corbusier says, "We won't really enter into modern urbanism without taking this prior decision: ...the corridor street must be destroyed."[56]

55. Elia, "Toward an Imperial City," in Ciucci, et al., *The American City*.

56. Le Corbusier, *Precisions on the State of Architecture and Urbanism* (Cambridge, Mass.: The MIT Press, 1991), 169.

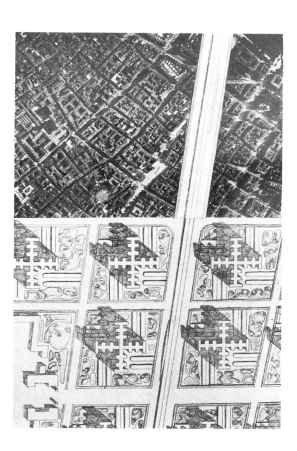

## SCENE 5
# The Modernist City

Modernist urbanism also defines itself as a reaction against the Baroque strategy of piercing that implies maintaining the existing medieval fabric. The tabula rasa is the point of departure for the modernist city of object buildings that do not form street walls and, as such, it will eliminate the existing fabric (and therefore the corridor streets) to allow for this new formal mutation. This will create an "American" condition, an empty ground fantasized as a "green" field where, in contrast with the corridor street, the modern street will be a new organ. "As a traffic machine . . . a sort of factory for producing street traffic the contemporary street presents itself in a totally new way. We walk under the trees, we see in the distance gigantic crystal weightless masses reflecting the sky, that seem to float. The pedestrians move on multilevel elevated streets, where they shop, sit on cafes and their gaze finds charming architectural works emerging from a sea of trees."[57]

Modernist urbanism is the fantasy that allows the European architect to deal with a new unattainable object of desire at the beginning of the twentieth century: the American city as a symptom of the modern city. Modernist urbanism is an ideology never realized, that went far on paper and became a poorly edited version in the built reality of the post–World War II period in Europe. Ville Contemporaine, one of the first of these fantasies, best illustrates this conflictive relationship to the desired object.[58] The project was organized around the three basic notions that structure the modern American city: a field conceived as a natural-ground (land) where the object-buildings are placed to avoid the creation

57. Ibid.

58. Le Corbusier, *The City of To-morrow and Its Planning* (reprint, New York: Dover, 1986).

of "dark street corridors"; a gridded plan of roads (without mentioning the Jeffersonian precedent); and the Cartesian skyscraper where the "youthful and passionate" original energy[59] of the American skyscraper is suppressed and transformed through Cartesian reason. This city was built in different modified versions going from the impoverished to the grotesque. World War II in Europe and the politics of urban renewal in America razed and killed the old city and its fabric, creating the tabula rasa that provided the "natural" ground where the modernist buildings were placed.

Le Corbusier's critique of Camillo Sitte and the corridor street obscures the fact that the question of the formal nature of the street is proposed by them in relation to two very different objects of study, and therefore developed within two very different problematics. While Sitte's object is the reinstatement of *public space* in the contemporary city, Le Corbusier's object is the mutation of the contemporary city into *architecture*.[60] While Sitte proposes an analysis of the formal conditions of European public space in the medieval and classical cities as a basis for returning to those spaces, the objective of Le Corbusier's criticism is the development of theoretical models and a specific architecture for the city in the "machine age."

Le Corbusier's critique of Sitte's position produced a powerful "side effect" — it implicitly established an opposition that will last for most of the twentieth century. "Public space" versus "the architectural city" are locked into mutually exclusive positions. The form of "public space" is seen as produced exclusively by the mechanisms at work in the classical city, as figural space, as roomlike configurations. The effect of the opposition is to universalize a European configuration of public space that needs to be historicized. On the other hand, the contemporary city, particularly in its street system and in its buildings, is seen as exclusively abstract and incompatible with figural space. While Sitte proposes a non-architectural Eurocentric conception of public space, Le Corbusier proposes a public space as a homogeneous "plastic" and architectural fact.

*The possibility of an-Other configuration of public space, defined as a transformation or mutation of the given formal conditions of public space, does not inform the European discourse.* The "given" formal conditions (the ones that were being explored by the American city) are suppressed by Le Corbusier who is looking into the "future," and by Sitte who is looking toward the "past."

The displacement of the concepts developed by the critique to retinal art in the 1990s[61] to the field of architecture could help us find the concepts to criticize modernist urbanism and make visible the American city as a reality that challenges what we are meant to "see" as architecture, that challenges the conditions of architectural seeing. We could start to "see" the particular behavior of its plan, the independence of the buildings, and the need to redefine not just the architectural configuration of public space but the way in which we conceptualize it.

While Le Corbusier suppresses the American city in his practice, Colin Rowe suppresses the American city in his theory fifty years

59. Le Corbusier, *The Radiant City: Elements of a Doctrine of Urbanism to Be Used as the Basis of Our Machine-age Civilization*, Pamela Knight, et al., trans. (London: Faber, 1967).

60. Le Corbusier, *Precisions on the State of Architecture and Urbanism*.

61. See Martin Jay, *Downcast Eyes* (Berkeley: University of California Press, 1993); Rosalind Krauss, *The Optical Unconscious* (Cambridge, Mass.: The MIT Press, 1993). This critique has allowed us to "see" "another" artistic production developed in an oblique way with respect to modernism. In particular the work of Duchamp is "illuminating" in its critique of opticality, of the notion of "creativity," in his discovery of the ready-made, and in his emphasis on reception.

FAR LEFT: Le Corbusier's Ville Contemporaine

LEFT: Place des Vosges, Paris

RIGHT: Mies van der Rohe's Lake Shore Drive buildings, Chicago

later.[62] The architectural critique of what was seen in the 1970s as the failure of modernist architecture (of its *formal* ambition to create a new city, of its *social* ambition to contribute to the improvement of the conditions of housing) was constructed on the basis of a representation that inverts in the plan the reading of what is figure and what is ground. The figure-ground diagrams were used by Rowe to explain the difference between the classical and the modernist European city while ignoring the American city. However, Rowe's figure-ground drawings miss their target when applied to the modernist European city because they project the classical city into the modernist city, suppressing its sectional aspirations (for instance, the difference between the Cartesian skyscrapers, the set-back buildings, and the *immeubles-villas*). At the same time, Rowe misses the potential of the figure ground for the analysis of the American city — which he describes in condescending terms — where the plan is independent of section, where they are useful as a first step into the depiction of the specificity of the America urban plan.

## ARCHITECTURE INHABITS THE CITY

Modernist architecture — and, by implication, the modernist city — traveled to America with the "International Style" exhibition at the Museum of Modern Art in New York City, and was established by the book of the same name by Russell Hitchcock and Philip Johnson.[63] But the modernist city does not take hold until after the Second World War when the business districts in the American city start to transform

under the influence of Mies van der Rohe's conception of the skyscraper (the Seagram building in New York City and the Lake Shore Drive buildings in Chicago, as opposed to his 1929 Berlin skyscraper). There are several factors that explain the favorable reception in America of the modernist city. The most obvious one is the openness to new configurations that characterized America since colonial times. However, another factor is that tabula rasa, which in America is a condition for development to take place, is also one of the most important conditions of the modernist city.

Europe opens up to the modernist city only after the Second World War produces a major tabula rasa. However, while in the 1950s the modernist city as a model is relegated to the suburbs, the American version of the modernist city, the one that will complement the suburban city, becomes the model for the business districts in Paris in the 1960s and 1970s (La Defense), in London in the 1980s (the Docklands), and in Shanghai in the 1990s (Pudong).

62. Colin Rowe and Fred Koetter, *Collage City* (Cambridge, Mass.: The MIT Press, 1978).

63. Russell Hitchcock and Philip Johnson, *The International Style* (New York: W. W. Norton, 1996).

## SCENE 6
# The Suburban City

The Interstate Highway Act of 1956 produces a radical change in the speed of development of the suburbs and in the articulation of suburban and urban environments. The Highway Act was implemented through a national network of roads that promoted the dominance of the car as the favored means of transportation and, as a consequence, brought the demise of public transportation. This dominance, in turn, accelerated the decline of pedestrian, exterior, public space and the growth of a generalized interior urban-suburban environment. The process of sub-urbanization, involving the systematic growth of fringe areas at a pace more rapid than that of the core city, produced in a few years a new urban mutation: the *suburban city*. This new urban form was defined in oppositional terms: the suburbs (as the positive term), versus the "down-town" or core city (as the negative term), the residential areas versus the workplace, white middle class versus black underclass. For the first time, the urban scene is conceived not as one complex stage, but as two opposing stages (urban/suburban) viewed from the "crabgrass frontier"[64] that separates the suburban city from a "wilderness" that keeps losing ground to the expanding city.

The *suburban city* was made possible by the industrialization of the *single-family house* and the *car* and it was overdetermined by national financing programs, by the redistribution of jobs necessary to employ the veterans of World War II, and by the physical construction of the high-way system. The Depression-born program of home-financing guarantee represented a first attempt to give the single-family house a prominent

64. Kenneth T. Jackson, *Crabgrass Frontier: The Suburbanization of the United States* (New York: Oxford University Press, 1985).

65. Dolores Hayden, *Redesigning the American Dream* (New York: W. W. Norton, 1984).

66. See Jackson, *Crabgrass Frontier*, 21–5.

67. Jackson, *Crabgrass Frontier*.

68. Andrew Jackson Downing, *A Treatise on the Theory and Practice of Landscape Gardening: Adapted to North America* (reprint, Washington, D.C.: Dumbarton Oaks Research Library and Collection, 1991). The book, based on English garden design principles, is proposed as an "American theory of architectural and garden design for a democratic society."

LEFT: Los Angeles freeway

RIGHT: automobile advertisement; television advertisement

status after World War I. However, the suburban city was only realized after World War II with the convergence of two factors, one social, the other physical. The first occurred when the employment of veterans and removal of women from the paid labor force became a national priority.[65] But the definitive impetus came from the construction of the interstate highway system, which had an essential role in producing a radical change in the form and speed of the development of suburban communities and the core city.

The *suburbs*, as residential districts of single-family houses built outside the city, were established in Boston, Philadelphia, and in New York[66] well before the Revolutionary War. The suburb, as a lifestyle separating and distancing the workplace from the residence and involving a daily commute to jobs in the center, can be dated to around 1815.[67] Symbolically, "the house in the country" for which Andrew Jackson Downing had written his theory of landscape gardening in the mid-nineteenth century, is the signifier that represents the contradiction between the forces of restlessness, movement, and migration and the local attachment to domestic life inherent in American culture.[68] This separation produced a new urban condition when the commuters (mostly men) went to work in the city driving cars on the new expressways built after World War II while their families stayed in the suburbs. According to Kenneth Jackson, four (positive) features defined the identity of these suburbs: class, location, home ownership, and density. Affluent and middle-class Americans started to move to suburban areas that were far from

work (and therefore dependent upon transportation) into homes they owned with yards that were enormous compared to the courtyards and backyards of the "walking city." Lower density and larger average lot size as compared with anything ever previously experienced in an urban world had been the effect of the car since the period between the wars. This effect increased exponentially after the establishment of the interstate highway system.[69]

The suburb can be seen as a moment of dynamic stability in a society of migrants and immigrants where the single-family house plays a crucial role. The oscillation between urban and antiurban ideologies[70] (and in the related antagonism between city and nature and house and city) has a direct effect on the objecthood of the single-family dwelling: when *nature* is seen as negative, *city* wins over the house that tends to become attached to the urban fabric. The new articulation of the house with nature provided by the *lawn* establishes a new structure that allows for the unattached house to be seen in the context of the antiurban tradition. The house itself is changed — gone are the two-story structures with parlor and porches. Frank Lloyd Wright's prairie houses are one-story servantless houses with no parlor, with carports and large expanses of glass instead of porches. The architectural "styles" as signs of permanence produce the *individuation* of the mass-produced type and *add weight* (the weight of history) to the wood-frame structures.[71]

The basic role of the detached single-family house was to produce the domestic construction of a family where women were full-time

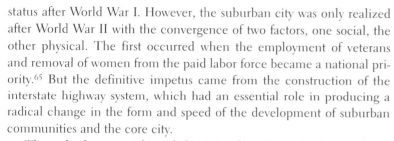

69. Jackson, *Crabgrass Frontier*. The density went from 20,000 per square mile in steetcar districts to 10,000 in the suburbs, which had lots ranging in size from 3,000 to 5,000 square feet.

70. Diana Agrest, et al., *The Sex of Architecture* (New York: Harry N. Abrams, 1996).

71. *Ladies Home Journal* offers plans for houses costing from $1,500 to $5,000 with full building specifications, together with estimates from four builders in different parts of the United States for $5.00 a set.

72. See Hayden, *Redesigning the American Dream*, 51.

homemakers and men absent breadwinners.[72] Domestic appliances transformed the domestic realm into a full-time workspace for women. Television, as the center of this new suburban home, assumed the crucial cultural and ideological functions of representing family life and supplemening the role of the traditional media in forming the new educated consumer. However, television played a more important urban function than its domestic role. In the *suburban fantasy*, television worked in tandem with the car to reestablish the connection lost by the movement away from the downtown. *The car supplemented the house and the television supplemented the city*, to which the single-family house becomes a crucial component. The car extends the house into the city, the television extends the city and its culture towards the house, which becomes the site where the viewer-consumer of the 1950s is systematically constructed. In some cases they supplant what they originally supplemented. The car finally becomes the house (as in the mobile home); the television becomes the city because it absorbs so many hours of viewing that family visits to the city become rare.

The advent of the car accelerates the decline of public transportation and open public space, and generates an interiorized urban/suburban environment. This is the beginning of the urban "fishbowl" that will dominate the contemporary X-Urban city. Commuters flow from air-conditioned, suburban, single-family houses by air-conditioned cars to air-conditioned offices; they have lunch in air-conditioned restaurants, go back to their offices and at the end of the day drive back to their homes. During their leisure time they will go shopping in air-conditioned malls and occasionally to air-conditioned multiplex cinemas.

A very early development, Radburn, New Jersey, designed in 1928 by Clarence Stein, became one of the most influential models for the suburban city. The plan overlapped a structure of *superblocks*, defined by secondary collector roads connected by main roads to the express highways, and a *garden city*, a picturesque plan with winding services lanes. This plan organized the suburban field, establishing an oppositional structure: the grid versus winding road, the natural landscape versus the mechanistic order, respect for the natural contour (harmonizing the site with the character of the land) versus the formal layout, English natural picturesque versus continental geometric order. Within this structure, the grid mediates the "organic" shapes of the lanes and the highway, the local scale and the regional scale; this seems to be the role of the new grid in the suburban city, a role that it already plays in Los Angeles. As opposed to the "classical" American city, which is spatially organized by the gridded plan meeting or intersecting the continental grid, the suburb is structured as a field where two sets of "organic" shapes related to two different speeds (the fast movement of the freeway system and the slow movement of the suburban developments) meet. The freeway system occupies the successive and almost coincident traces of the railroad dating back to the early Native American trails, a system that condenses history and geography, in the search for a smooth and constant flow. The suburbs themselves are organized by means of a pattern of curvilinear street patterns that intends to slow down the movement and shorten the views, and dead-ends where the movement finally stops.

While architects such as Stein will play a role in suburban development, the architect's place is going to be eliminated in the production or the suburban city.[73] It is still too soon to know if a site could be built for the architect's intervention in future rewritings of the suburban city, the way in which they are taking place, for instance, in France where postwar suburban developments are now being restructured.

The *morphology* of the suburban city cannot be depicted with the opposition fabric versus object, which describes the major formal difference between the classical city (or city of fabric) and the modernist city (or city of objects). Although the suburban city has a resemblance to the modernist city, in its preponderance of voids and in that the solids appear as objects in a field, it presents a characteristic that establishes a similarity to the classical city. Because the field is divided into similar lots and the houses present typological similarities, we read it as texture, as a discontinuous fabric as opposed to the continuous texture of the classical city. The suburban city proposes a situation that blurs and subverts the fabric/object opposition with a condition that could be called *object as fabric*.

The fabric of the core also undergoes a transformation. The deterioration produced by the middle-class flight to the suburbs, along with the operations of urban renewal, produces a new condition that could be called "fabric as object." The "white flight" to the suburbs changes the

73. According to the design guidelines, the federal agency responsible for funding would penalize any builder who hired an "architect" by lowering the mortgageable value that did not conform to their design regulations (e.g., flat roofs). Gwendolyn Wright, *Building the Dream: A Social History of Housing in America* (New York: Pantheon, 1981), 247–8.

LEFT: Hartford, Connecticut, 1953, before urban renewal; Hartford, Connecticut, 1965, after urban renewal

NEAR RIGHT: Mies van der Rohe's Seagram building, New York City, 1954–8

FAR RIGHT: Robert Venturi's A Bill-Ding-Board for the National Football Hall of Fame Competition, 1967

RIGHT INSET: Mies van der Rohe's IIT campus, Chicago, 1941

demographic character of the *downtown* and starts the process of its deterioration. Planners predicted that the explosion of communications and media would promote the dissolution of the high-density physical city[74] and the disappearance of free, twenty-four-hour accessible, and nonpoliced public space. Because the intraurban network of roads was better than the interurban transportation, the cities began to come apart economically (middle and upper class versus lower class) and functionally (residential versus commercial). This only reinforced the process of coming apart that separated the downtown and the suburbs, a process that started with the breakdown of the annexation of the new suburban enclaves and prepared the ground for the emergence of a new urban mutation, the X-Urban city.

## ARCHITECTURE INHABITS THE "CORE" OF THE SUBURBAN CITY

Two architectural fantasies are projected onto the suburban city, compensating for the lack of intervention in the reality of this city. The first, the center city, is best represented by Mies van der Rohe's American period. Coming from the past, from the first modernism, Mies's projects in the late 1940s and 1950s, the modernist architectural city is projected onto the American city. The Seagram complex on Park Avenue in New York City "pushes" the building back providing a reading of "the building as object on a podium" as seen from a car. On the side streets, the building crashes against a lower "fabric" forming a street wall. With the Seagram building, Mies stages a modernist city (a city of objects) on the avenue, juxtaposed to the nonarchitectural city of fabric of the side streets. A new scopic regime, described by Mies in a 1932 article[75] proposing two visual registers determined by speed preannounces this strategy. Mies opposes a view determined by the speed of the car, where the expressways will "unlock new landscapes," not just rural but also urban, not just of vegetation but of advertising, to the classical pedestrian viewpoint. While the slow reading of architecture is reserved to the pedestrian, the car allows for a new view of the *landscape*. The opposition "pedestrian versus car" in Mies's urban projects — the pedestrian field of objects in the Illinois Institute of Technology campus and the Seagram plaza — allows for the definition of two different speeds that oppositionally define the new scopic regime.

## THE SUBURBAN CITY INHABITS ARCHITECTURE

The second architectural fantasy concerns the suburban city proper. The architectural effect of this urban mutation is best staged by Venturi's work; Venturi's texts in the mid-1960s and in the early 1970s present a retroactive gaze that looks back to the 1950s.[76] It is all about the car, and therefore about the suburban city. The oppositions "driver versus pedestrian" and "landscape versus architecture" are now seen as an attempt to domesticate the forces unleashed by the car: architecture is made the equivalent of advertising images[77] that conceal utilitarian structures or "sheds." The billboard and the sign are the critical weapons that,

74. See in particular Melvin Webber's communicational approach, "The Misfortunes of Theory," in Agrest, *Architecture from Without*.

75. Mies van der Rohe, "Expressways as an Artistic Problem," *Die Autobahn* 5 (1932). In this very short text, Mies describes the basic notions that will be structured theoretically by Venturi thirty years later in his *Complexity and Contradiction in Architecture*.

76. Venturi, *Complexity and Contradiction in Architecture*.

77. There is a reference to pop art in Venturi's work.

78. The dominance of the image and surface explains the abandonment of both classical urban space and the modernist notion of the field as ground where the "symphony of shapes" is being played. See Le Corbusier, *Precisions on the State of Architecture and Urbanism*. "Disneyfication" could be seen as the development of this ideology into the imagineering of the themed urban places of the 1990s.

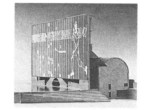

together with the notions of complexity and contradiction, deal a blow to the apparently exhausted modernist ideology. This is another example of a job not completely finished: modernism is "buried alive," or not properly buried through critical work. Venturi repeats modernism's gesture when classical architecture was buried alive, which explains why their ghosts, both classical and modernist, keep coming back.[78]

## THE OBSTACLES TO ARCHITECTURE

The suburban city poses a major difficulty to architecture — it cannot simply be described in formal terms. It is neither about the architectural object nor about the plan. It is about the sign and particularly about its reception, that is, about the subject. This forces the reframing of the urban question. Therein lies the vision of Venturi, in the way he expands the definition of the city. Another major change results from Denise Scott Brown's introduction of the planner's critique to the architectural totalizing view of the city. From that point on architecture will be about "urban buildings," the total abandonment of classical urban space and its replacement with image, and the abandonment of both representation and abstraction and their replacement with simulacra.[79]

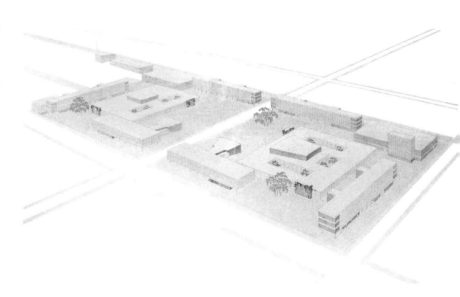

79. The Las Vegas of the 1990s brings back space as simulacrum — outdoor space along the model of the theme park and interior space as filmic stage set.

## SCENE X

# The Development of the X-Urban City

A new urban restructuring took place in the 1970s and acquired full speed in the 1980s, as expressions of the growth and the dominance of the service industry in general, and the globalization of the finance industry in particular. One of the symptoms of this process was the development of exurban "office campuses," which blurred the opposition of suburbs versus central city that had symbolically structured the suburban city. As part of the restructuring of the workplace, the white-collar workforce, which now included a high percentage of women, was moved to secondary offices in less expensive locations. The post–World War II suburbs that had been exclusively residential now became part of clusters including offices, shopping malls, and entertainment centers, where the new exurbanites could work, shop, and play. This change defines a new multiuse urbanity, with a very low density and a total dependence on the automobile. X-Urbia (*Ex*: out of; *exurbia*: out of the city) has transformed America into a colossal urbanized territory.[80] Where are these new developments located? Besides the office campuses, most of the new housing is being developed in the outer edges of the suburban city, in the one-mile grid or in the intersections of the freeway system.

The semiautonomy of these urban clusters provides them with a certain independence from the core city, which becomes one more semiautonomous urban "village" in the metropolitan constellation of X-Urban centers. However, this process of "sprawl" accounts for only one side of the X-Urban city. In the downtowns of the old cities,

80. Mario Gandelsonas, "Conditions for a Colossal Architecture," in *Cesar Pelli: Buildings and Projects 1965–1990* (New York: Rizzoli, 1990).

LEFT: Aerial view of Des Moines, Iowa

RIGHT: Microsoft Campus, Redmond, Washington

the exclusive light industrial districts also experience a transformation through processes of gentrification and preservation. While the processes of "voiding" the residential buildings from the center city continued, buildings in light industrial districts were gentrified; that is, transformed into residential buildings and with that came new shopping and entertainment repeating the X-Urban processes in the edges of the metropolitan area. In other words, the gentrification of decayed neighborhoods and light industrial districts, and the X-Urbanization of residential suburban areas into a car-dependent, low-density urbanity, are two sides of the same coin. In both cases, the major apparent changes occur at the level of programming while there seems to be very little visible change at the physical and formal level.

However, a major change takes place in downtowns throughout America at a morphological level: fields of parking, with object-buildings and/or fragments of urban fabric sitting on them become the dominant landscape. The freeway also enters and disrupts the downtowns, producing urban fields of parking and isolated object-buildings and/or islands of fabric. The city of Des Moines, Iowa, is one of hundreds of cities where the downtown has become an office park where commuters that live in exurbia work. A very dense and compact downtown business district where clusters of office buildings and parking structures are linked in this particular case with a hermetic skywalk system, is surrounded by over one hundred acres of parking on ground. The persistence of these dense downtowns have falsified the predictions of the

1960s planners about the disappearance of the city: the downtowns grow more during the 1980s than in any period since the end of World War II[81]. The economic restructuring of the 1980s requires both the dense downtown business districts and the sparse X-Urban office campuses.

The changes brought by the X-Urban city define a new urbanity not organized anymore in oppositional terms such as center versus periphery but as a multicenter city, not as a dominant totality versus subordinated parts but as a nonhierarchical fragmented urbanized territory. While all the other mutations entertain an oppositional relationship with the previous cities, the current mutation is developing by contiguity to the urban/suburban city. As such, the X-Urban city supplements the suburban city programmatically but also supplants the previous city. This new city is something added to make up for a deficiency; for instance, major European cities lack massive, structured, touristic consumption, a shortcoming that is remedied by their conversion to theme parks such as the Parisian Louvre. However this addition ends up taking the place of the previous city, which in turn is integrated as part of the theme parks or as neutral, picturesque or invisible background. For example, in Battery Park City in Manhattan, Wall Street becomes a background for a space that collapses and brings together gentrified and X-Urban space. The changes affect not just the city but also the buildings nor just the exterior but also their interiors, redefine and multiply the public and the private spheres and displace the public space into the house and the private space into the streets.[82]

81. See Sassen, *The Global City*.

The X-Urbia of the 1990s is produced by the *condensation* of the programs left behind by the suburban city (the workplace and entertainment), located in "points," in the proximity of existing or new residential X-Urban neighborhoods. Office campuses and multiplex cinemas come to the suburbs, transforming them into disjointed or scattered cities with the car as the predominant mode of transportation. The suburbs of the 1950s, the scattered neighborhoods of the suburban city, have not changed; they become older and start to decay. They become one of the elements of the new X-Urban scattered city.

The old city center, the urban city, and exurbia are depicted in terms of two opposing *fantasies: the urban fantasy and the X-Urban fantasy.* In the latter "edge city," one of the names given to X-Urbia, is seen as a necessary stage in the process of urban growth, an economic inevitability. While the center city is seen as an impossible condition, the very picture of present disaster, edge city is described as a green Edenic space. Urbanism, associated with tall buildings and "too much asphalt," is worst than parking lots.[83] While edge city is structured around the individual freedom, the go-anywhere provided by the car, the center city depends on the less desirable centralized mode of transportation of mass transit.[84] What this view suppresses is the question of government support that sustains the X-Urban development.[85] In the former fantasy, the center, seen as the repository of history, identity, diversity, and the realm of culture, stands in opposition to X-Urbia, which is determined solely by economics. The condition of the center is attributed to its relationship

(or lack thereof) with suburbia. The sprawl, where X-Urbia flourishes, is where the blame is placed. The metaphor of the wall depicts both conditions, "cramming the poor into the constricted center cities, while the suburbs maintain its wall of segregation," or "boundaries that cordon off the core city from the suburban territory."[86] While edge city is presented in a negative way, leading towards some future environmental and social catastrophe, the center city is seen as a "possible future" in the development of the megalopolis. This prediction of a "possible future" is supported by the fact that opening those walls to produce the interdependence of city-suburbs exurbs produces positive results: the better center-city incomes compare to the suburbs the better the economic regional performance.[87] And the way to make this happen is by systematically annexing new growth areas and creating cities without suburbs.

Both fantasies deny the contingent, the violent emergence of something that defies the limits of the established field, the limits of what one holds for "possible," where possible is, so to speak, a pacified contingency. An example of this contingency is the entrance of women into the labor market and its effects, which marks the end of the suburban fantasy and the beginning of the X-Urban fantasy. This fact, the new role played by women, shattered the stability of the suburban order, exposing the repressed antagonism in the fixed gender roles structured by the suburban fantasy, and produced the conditions for the emergence of the X-Urban city. This fact never figured into the planning "theories" and

82. The changes also affect the field of vision: different computer techniques such as computer-aided design and animation, virtual-imaging helmets, and magnetic resonance imaging destabilize the notion of representation and relocate vision by separating it from the human observer. Today vision is situated in an electromagnetic terrain of bits as opposed to both classical perception and the twentieth-century analog media such as photography, film, and television.

83. Joel Garreau, *Edge City: Life on the New Frontier* (New York: Doubleday, 1991), 45.

84. However the question is not just about private versus public transportation but about the eruption of desire in relation to movement and transportation, which was essentially functional since the days when walking and horseback riding were the primary modes of transportation.

85. National laws for taxation, highways, and environmental protection favor the suburbs.

86. Neal R. Peirce, *Citistates: How Urban America Can Prosper in a Competitive World* (Santa Ana, Calif.: Seven Locks Press, 1993), 119.

87. Ibid., 19.

LEFT: World Financial Center, New York City

INSET: Cesar Pelli and Associates, Pacific Design Center, Los Angeles

RIGHT: SoHo, New York City

predictions of the 1960s. We are now facing an unexpected massive entrance into the virtual city and the possibilities of active participation (in commercial rather than political activities) given by the World Wide Web. With these possibilities come the opening of new opportunities, the emergence of new desires, of new unreachable objects that will affect urbanity in unexpected ways.

Kenneth Jackson establishes a continuity between suburbia and exurbia, exurbia as an intensification of suburbia in a view that looks at the urban/suburban dichotomy as a stable relationship where the two terms complement each other, where the positive and negative signs alternate; for instance, when the contemporary situation is seen as a reversal of the flight to the suburbs, a "back-to-downtown," which is his desire. However, neither the 1980s downtown nor the suburbs are the same as the original terms of the suburban city. One could actually reverse Jackson's theory and propose the suburban city as a transitory stage of the X-Urban city in the process that starts with the gridding of America.[88]

"Scene X" or "X-Urbia," which is being constructed and multiplied while I write, is a scene where two similar objects, the television set and the computer monitor, which belong to two different systems, analogic versus digital, define two different cities, the suburban and the exurban. Television became the window[89] that allowed the view of the urban city and brought it to the suburban city and is now being challenged and perhaps superseded by the computer monitor's opening of X-Urbia to the global city, erasing national boundaries and consolidating the X-Urban fantasy. However, while national boundaries are being blurred, local boundaries are being built. The process of destabilization of the sub urban city and the emergence of the X-Urban city was overdetermined by the development of a black middle class that started to move into the suburbs, blurring the oppositions city versus suburbs correlated to the opposition black versus white. A new fantasy fuels the centrifugal impulse

88. Jackson, *Crabgrass Frontier*.

89. Thomas Keenan, "Windows of Vulnerability," in Bruce Robbins, ed., The Phantom Public Space (Minneapolis: University of Minnesota Press, 1993), 121–41.

exploited by the developers of the newest X-Urban gated communities: *the suburbs are now the stage where crime takes place.*

Gated communities are the new X-Urban armored residential developments being built at the outer edges of the megacities throughout America insulated from the outside with implied or sometimes literal walls. These paranoid exurban walls are opposed to the ecological walls or boundaries that the urbanites want to impose in the constantly expanding process of *sprawl*.[90]

These changes are taking place not only at the level of the urban object but also (and perhaps primarily) at the level of the urban subject, a subject defined by the X-Urban city. It is through an example born of the transformation of the suburban residential areas from imaginary suburban landscapes into a territory of imaginary violence that we can begin the construction of this subject. This example is not about the way in which these spaces are configured, but rather about the way in which these spaces are perceived though the media, specifically as seen through the television program *Cops*.[91]

*Cops* is a television show that airs daily and presents itself as a documentary. Each episode is structured around three events located in different cities. During each event the camera follows a team of police officers from the point when they are about to apprehend a criminal. Although the action is not staged, the program is rigorously edited and constructed. For instance, the action always takes place in the suburbs, of which an aerial view is shown in the presentation. First, the camera inside the car alternates between the profile of the cop driving his car while explaining the "case," and the view from behind the windshield where the viewer is placed in the position of the cop. The scene where the criminal is subject to police intervention usually takes place in X-Urban terrain (trailer parks and other deteriorated suburban environments), or inside a suburban house or apartment building. The suburbs are now the stage where crime takes place. The criminals are mostly white, lower-middle-class suburbanites involved in drugs and violence; most often the programs are about domestic disputes, which stand in sharp contrast to the 1950s depiction of family life.

What is interesting about *Cops* is that we find in the 1990s the same elements that define the suburbia of the 1950s: the suburban *house*, the *car*, the *television*. However these elements are articulated in two very different series of equivalencies. In the first situation, the 1950s suburb, the car and the TV represent the drastic restructuring of relations between private/public and interior/exterior that differentiates suburbia from the classical city: the emphasis on privatization and interiorization. While the car becomes the extension of the house and the windshield becomes a new type of (private) window that frames the exterior (public) space, the television screen acts as the gate for the public to invade the interior domestic space.

While in the 1950s suburban city, the car and the television are different means to *see*, for *viewing*, in the 1990s the exurban observer is *being seen*. In *Cops*, the car represents the eye of the law, and the tele-

90. The exurban city is the physical manifestation of a process that produces constantly expanding boundaries.

91. This television show was the research topic chosen by Joseph Cho, a graduate student in my urbanism seminar at the Princeton University School of Architecture in Princeton, New Jersey.

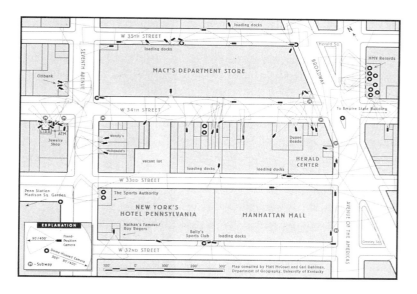

vision frames the house. While the suburban observer is defined as a driver, through the windshield viewing at a certain speed, in contrast to the slow pace of pedestrian urban observer of the classical city, the X-Urban observer, a *subject* who can travel through electronic space at any time, who zaps through hundreds of television channels and surfs the World Wide Web, is defined at the same time as the *object* of constant surveillance.

The technological-political changes of the 1990s transform private space, which is now increasingly constituted by a mechanism (telephone-fax-email-Internet) that augments and extends the fluid circulation of private information. However, there is a painful paradox in the coextensivity of the democratization of information and of the field of the police and the state: the extension of the power of the police parallels the democratic permeability and transparency of personal communication. The same technology that constitutes and circumscribes a new privately controlled space is the same that opens it up to intrusion.[92]

The practice of surveillance affects the boundaries between public and private: they become transparent. Furthermore, this practice does not just affect the existing fixed spatial boundaries. The permanent flow of the police car produces a mobile temporal boundary, an implied wall pierced by the horizontal windows produced by the movement of the car. This implied wall that the police surveillance produces in the suburbs is correlated to the literal wall of the new X-Urban armored communities that are being built at the outer edges of megacities throughout America.

Why this pathological return of the wall? At the imaginary level, the wall is a defensive gesture, a reaction to X-Urban violence. Since the private is violated or fantasized as such, the privatizing reaction that follows (familial, nationalizing, ethnocentric) is expected.[93] However, while these walls are useless, or always subject to actual or visual piercing in reality, they fulfill a role at a fantasy level and at the same time they indicate a new articulation of the symbolic field in X-Urbia. While

92. Jacques Derrida, "Questions d'Etranger," in *Anne Dufourmantelle Invite Jacques Derrida a Repondre, de l'Hospitalite* (Paris: Calman-Levy, 1997), 57.

93. Ibid., 51. See also M. Christine Boyer, *Cybercities: Visual Perception in the Age of Electronic Communication* (New York: Princeton Architectural Press, 1996).

LEFT: Hong Kong's central business district

INSET: development in Arizona

the symbolic world of the suburban city is structured in terms of the separation and reconnection of city and suburb, of the urban and suburban cities, the X-Urban city problematizes the (ever-extending) object's edge, the subject's gaze. While the connecting suburban mechanisms (the car, the TV) transforms the private/public /-/interior/exterior relationships, the marking of boundaries in the X-Urban city transforms the private/public /-/actual/virtual relationships.

From an architectural point of view, the symbolic role of these walls might be the marking and the materialization on the vertical plane of what is lacking on the horizontal plane. The continuing expansion of the megacity brings up the question of the edge, the lack of an edge, and, at the symbolic level, the return of the frontier as a major signifier that replaces the garden, the major signifier in the suburban city. Since sprawl blurs the edge of the megacity, the marking of edges becomes an obsession: gated communities, urban frontiers,[94] bounded natural preserves. While the suburban relation is internal to the city (urban-suburban) the frontier that separates civilization from savagery (that is, unruly uncooperative nature[95]), is present in different ways in the urban, the suburban, and the X-Urban. The frontier in the city is established between the "inner city population" as a "natural element" and the gentrifying forces of "urban pioneers" that advance on the basis of internal differentiation of an existing fabric. In the suburbs the frontier is established by circulating police cars that construct the imaginary safety wall in the television docudrama *Cops*. And, in X-Urbia, the frontier is materialized with the wall (literal or imaginary) of the new communities that separate them from the external world and that are populated with wild animals instead of urban or suburban pets: crocodiles in Florida, deer and foxes in New York and New Jersey, and dangerous insects such as deer ticks (that attack the body) instead of suburban termites (that attack the house).

The walls are perhaps the result of a symbolic identification with downtown, the place without literal walls (or material walls, as with the Internet). They are the return on the vertical plane of what is lacking in the horizontal plane; they are the return in the material world of what is lacking in the virtual world. The wall of surveillance, as we know can both protect but also invade our privacy. In the X-Urban city, the two possibilities given by centralized surveillance or generalized access to surveillance define two very different models: the scary one where police control surveillance, or the other, proposed by *Cops*, as a fantasy where the police themselves are always potentially subject to surveillance, where the police are being watched.

## ARCHITECTURE INHABITS THE CITY

While the 1970s were most notably dedicated to theoretical production, the 1980s were about building with many urban-scale projects being initiated, particularly in Europe (Paris, Barcelona, Berlin), but also in Asia. However these interventions are still designed in the spirit of early modernism or a postmodernism that ignores the X-Urban city. In fact, most architecture ignores the X-Urban city.

94. Urban frontiers protect the gentrified areas from the neighboring slums. See Neil Smith, *The New Urban Frontier: Gentrification and the Revanchist City* (New York and London: Routledge, 1996).

95. Smith, *The New Urban Frontier*.

## THE CITY INHABITS ARCHITECTURE

The fact that the "architecturally resistant" X-Urban city is spreading — not only across the American territory, but across the world — opens up a problematic concerning both the city and architecture that has not yet been theorized: the question of the identity of the American city, the role that architecture plays in its construction and the related questions concerning architecture's insistence in this role or, in other terms, the city's persistent role as the object of architecture.

While the suburban city proposed a spatial opposition between two types of cities — one, European and classical, the other, American and modern — the X-Urban city proposes a relationship to the previous American urban mutations that takes place both in the temporal as well as in the spatial dimension. While expanding the definition of the city, the X-Urban city appears as the latest stage in a process of construction of urban identity that involves the three previous American cities: the gridded city, the city of skyscrapers, and the suburban city.

Since the X-Urban city rejects architecture the way we know it and, since architecture nevertheless insists on the possibility of an articulation with "the city" (a signifier for a different urban entity that has been radically restructured multiple times), the possible strategies for the articulation of architecture and the X-Urban city need to include a previous historization and theorization of their relationship that goes back to the constitutive moments of architecture itself.

# The Identity of the American City

The American city has been radically changing since World War II. Until only fifty years ago the configuration of the older American cities of the Northeast and of most of the downtowns in the rest of the country was very similar to the European city, in particular in the way their city blocks were extruded by defining, continuous, street walls. Although features such as the jagged skyline created by skyscrapers or the scale given by the high-rise prewar buildings in New York and Chicago made them quite unique, their *compact* fabric recalled various European lineages. Cities such as Los Angeles, characterized by a high percentage of scattered buildings, looked very different. However Los Angeles was a growing city and one could suppose that after a while it would follow the trend of the denser Eastern cities, and end up looking more like them. Nevertheless, the change in urban configuration brought by the process of suburbanization after the war established the *scattered* pattern as the rule and not the exception of the look of "younger" cities. Today, even in a city like New York, the construction of attached buildings is an exception — as in the case of Battery Park City, with its simulacrum of prewar urban fabric — and the scattered pattern is the rule. The very large structures built in the last ten years tend to be autonomous objects forced to make conciliatory gestures towards the sidewalk rather than explore new relationships with it.

This change from compact to scattered revealed something about the identity of the American city that was not apparent before. The scattered pattern, as one of the differential features that structure this identity, was obscured by the presence of the street walls in the American downtowns, which established an apparent similarity with the European city. One of the aspects where the European and American cities radically differ is in the problematic relationship between plan and buildings and between the buildings themselves.[1] In the American city the buildings never related strictly to the plan and tended to be independent from each other — even when they formed a street wall — to a degree where the scattered pattern was always potentially readable. (This is true even in the compressed pattern of the street wall, which lasted only for just over a century.) Opposingly, the attached quality of the extruded European urban fabric is reinforced by features such as strong horizontal cornices.[2] The suburban city, in realizing this potential to its full extent, represented the strongest and most effective attempt to reassert the different configuration of urban America.

1. The streets have also very different symbolic roles. While in Europe, streets have a secondary role with respect to squares, "Main Street" is the dominant public space in America. While in Europe, streets tend to become spaces, because of the typological uniformity of the street walls, in America they read as voids that suture the separation between blocks. While in Europe they have a mediating role, in America they represent a split. Whilshire Boulevard in Santa Monica, California, and a Parisian Haussmanian boulevard represent these two extreme conditions.

2. When the cornices travel to America they become "tops" accentuating the unique character of every structure, instead of the element that links individuals buildings and subsumes them into fabric.

The suburban city was perhaps the last chapter in the quest to constitute an urban identity, a pursuit that is integral to the history of the American city. This difficult process was developed through a complex play of similarity and difference with the European city[3] that activated the flow of urban configurations described in the previous chapter. This was a process characterized by two contradictory impulses: on one hand the establishment of an order through *identification*, evident in the inclination towards mimesis with the European city, and on the other hand the opposite impulse towards radical differentiation (*disidentification*) through the invention of new urban plans and building typologies as a way to produce a new urban identity. The "head" of Boston as opposed to its gridded "neck," and Manhattan before the establishment of the gridiron, are examples of the first case; the plan of Savannah, Georgia, and the skyscraper are examples of the second case.

The effect of this process was not felt only in the American city. As the *other* of Europe, America had a critical influence in the constitution of the identity of the cities on both sides of the Atlantic. The flows that linked them were not just a circuit of exchange but a space where a complex choreography defined by a play of desire and identification took place, where each side fantasized the other, where both Europe and America pursued different ways to constitute their identity. Europe's desire, the wish to *have* the other, defined its relationship to the Americas — politically, economically, and culturally — until the twentieth century. America's identification with Europe, the wish to *be* the

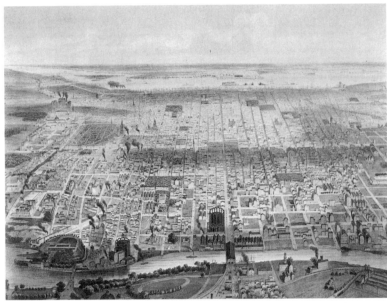

other,[4] defines the other side of an asymmetrical relationship. The cities became the three-dimensional constructions that materialized these fantasies in different ways: America as the virgin land, as the setting for the scene of the future, and Europe as the already-built land that worked as a cultural repository, as the memory of the past.[5] An example of this struggle is the antagonism between Louis Sullivan and Daniel H.

3. Identity can only be produced in a differential way: The cluster of its features, properties or qualities can only be recognized as difference (i.e, the gridded vs. the nongridded, the scattered vs. the attached, high-rise vs. low-rise, etc.).

4. Diana Fuss, *Identification Papers* (New York: Routledge, 1995), 11.

5. The fact that the European cities existed and the American cities did not does not imply that they simply opposed each other in terms of their identities. While the identity of the existing European city could be recognized as opposed to the American city where identity was to be produced, the European city changed in dramatic ways after the discovery of America and their configuration was restructured in a continuous process of identity production.

Burnham in Chicago at the end of the nineteenth century representing, respectively, a "new American architecture" in the margins of architectural language, and the desire to "beat Europe on its own ground" (that is, working within the European stylistic principles).

The establishment of the American settlements became, for Europe, an important first step in the process of management and control of the new colonies. The play of differences inscribed in the urban plan became embedded in pairs of oppositions that produced the identity of the colonial American city and consolidated the identity of the imperial European city. This discursive dimension was implemented in contemporary opposing urban realities: the large and totalizing American city plans projected onto "virgin" land (e.g., Philadelphia of 1684) versus the partial and localized urban European interventions carved in the existing fabric (e.g., Place des Victoires of 1685–87; Bloomsbury Square of 1661, before the Great Fire; and Grosvenor Square of 1720, after the Great Fire). The discursive dimension was also found in opposing formal approaches such as the American pragmatic two-dimensional grids such as the Detroit, Michigan, plan of 1701, versus the European ceremonial sequences of spaces such as Versailles (1661–1708).

Since the urban plans were very different, the buildings and the urban fabric became, for colonial America, the place where, through a play of similarity and transformation, an identification with the European city took place. The building of the structures provided the stage where the familiar images of the European towns could be reproduced through a play of distorting mirrors. The effect of the familiar image was one of misrecognition and concealment of its colonial status, of the radical difference between the configuration of the American urban plans (that represented the European colonial role and materialized its architectural urban fantasies) and the reality of the European cities (particularly, their plans and monuments).

Because from the beginning the New World was seen as an "empty space," an absence, the attempts to fill that void required for the European colonizer the establishment of an order. This is what produced the opening to architecture (whose role is precisely the institution of a formal order in buildings) as an adjutant in the foundation of the American city, as in the architectural order embedded in the Law of Indies, in the French Bastide plans, and in the English gridded urban plans. The role of architecture in the New World, its peculiar articulation with the American city, illuminated the very different roles that architecture played on the two sides of the Atlantic. In Europe, the relation between architecture and the existing city was always central to the production of the identity of architecture itself. In America, architecture played an initial role in the construction of the identity of the city (although mediated through political or economic institutions) and was later on relegated to the margins.

Architecture was not part of the constitutive moment of the European city (that is, the medieval city[6]), and becomes engaged with this physical city through the construction of fantasies. In Europe during the Renaissance, architecture encounters the medieval physical city, and its interventions proceed most times by "subtraction," in the design of voids rather than solids. It is in the European urban voids where architecture has found a site for its urban practice, in the public squares and in the streets. Instead, the configuration of the European city plan is the result of pure contingency, a result of the interaction of multiple economic and political forces. Alternatively, America provided a blank slate for the design of the plan of the city. While in America architecture came a priori, before the city was built, in Europe the architectural interventions took place a posteriori, after the city had been built. While in Europe the cities were punctuated with architectural buildings and spaces, in America architecture was disseminated throughout the city by the plan. Architecture's role was either a way to bring some order at the point of departure when politicians or entrepreneurs "invented" new plans for the city, or an introduction of order in a new typological experiment (such as the case of the skyscraper). In the late nineteenth century, Central Park in New York City represents a rare case of architectural intervention that went beyond the plan where a totalizing design is implemented. This broad, extensive relationship that is never complete, that always escapes the architect's control and desire of totality, has always been problematic for architecture.[7]

After American independence, the quest for identity acquires a new urgency. However, in America, architecture will not be the generator of the new radical urban fantasies as it was the case across the Atlantic where they inhabited the European Imaginary for centuries. The fantasies that will sustain the American pursuit of identity will be produced by architecturally informed politicians and entrepreneurs, while architects will be relegated most of the time to the margins. As a result of this displacement, the contradictory impulses towards mimesis and differentiation animating those fantasies will produce not just an architectural restructuring of urban configuration, but formal mutations that break away from the logic of architecture radically transforming the American city.

One of the features that characterized these post-Revolutionary American *urban fantasies* was their *unifying* impulse.[8] In that respect, urban fantasies paralleled the new *social fantasies* in their construction of a vision of a *unified* democratic society. While social fantasy provides a means to describe society as an undivided body — concealing the antagonistic divisions that traverse it and cannot be integrated into the symbolic order — urban fantasy allows us to depict the city as a correlated unified entity.[9]

In the case of the American social fantasy, the construction of the *unified* vision given by democracy was overdetermined by the necessity to deal with *external* and *internal* social divisions and antagonisms[10] — not just the ones coming from outside, from the multiple colonizations, but from inside, from the singularity and diversity of the different "Americas" after independence, from the plurality of geographies and in

6. Actually, architecture is constituted as a break with respect to the medieval building practices. See the Preface in Alberti, *Ten Books on Architecture*.

7. Washington, D.C., a city where architecture had a major role both at its inception and in its development, represents the exception to the rule.

8. This feature, which is also shared by the urban and architectural fantasies, might explain the convergence that took place with modernist urbanism desire for the American city. Despite the totalizing character of the architectural fantasies in Europe, the architect only *partially* realizes his desire. In America the city rejected the architect altogether and only in exceptional circumstances a possibility of realization seemed to come true; for instance, the white city of the 1892 Chicago Columbian exhibition, which was, however, a *temporary* structure, a mirage.

9. The role of social fantasy is to construct a vision of society that is not divided by antagonistic forces, a society in which the relation between its parts is complementary. See Slavoj Žižek, "How Did Marx Invent the Symptom?" in Slavoj Žižek, ed., *Mapping Ideology* (London and New York: Verso, 1994).

particular from the antagonistic cultures of what we call America.[11] The establishment of democracy implied the delimitation of boundaries separating what belonged to the order and its outside. These boundaries were at the same time necessary (they are the condition of existence for an order) and impossible in that they always fail to stop the process,of permanence differentiation by which society is permanently reconfigured (a process that explains the incomplete and open character of *social identity*).[12]

The different urban fantasies also played a unifying role: the one-mile grid establishes a relentless order through a pattern that ignores geographical difference; the skyscraper type provides a way to perceive again a city that escapes perception as a unified entity; the process of suburbanization spreads the equality of the single family house through the fluidity of the continuous road; and now the "electronic highway" — in particular, the pull technology of the World Wide Web — constructs a global public space where information, actively produced and exchanged, flows without barriers.[13]

The incomplete and open character that characterizes *urban identity* also becomes apparent in the process of development and change of the American city which has always been in transition. The major difficulty confronted by this process was that the different orders constituting the identity of the American city were constantly antagonized and threatened by the city itself: it was impossible to fix something (the city) that resisted fixing. How was this precarious urban identity constructed? Through the development of the three American urban mutations, of the successive urban fantasies where new operations configuring the physical territory take place. These operations relate to specific instances of the general process of urban development determined by political and economic forces. In every one of them a *major signifier* produces a radical restructuring of the symbolic field:

**1.** The frontier as a process of *expansion* of the national boundaries and a chain of actions and effects, the parallel process of surveying by means of the continental grid and the neutralization of geography, the unification of the extraordinary diversity and plurality of landscapes. The establishment of the *grid* (that is, of geometric similarity that suppresses difference) obscures the reality of America as an "assemblage" of disparate physical and social fragments, the mosaic held together by a network of communication and exchange, linking villages, towns, cities, and now megacities.

**2.** The centripetal process of *densification* of the city, the *skyscraper* and the construction/destruction of the city (the history actually starts here, with the invention of an "American" type, and the liberation of section from the plan reasserting the city as a collection of disparate buildings, a diversity initially denied by the gridded plan). The establishment (promotion) of freedom obscures class, race, and gender antagonisms.

10. The Union, which brought a political order that intended to overcome the divisions between the states, was accomplished at a great cost. The political implication was that the freedoms and the right to equality contained in the political imaginary of democracy from its inception were restricted to the white, Anglo-American sector of the population, a restriction that had vast spatial implications. The marks of this exclusion, which constantly return to haunt the apparently unified society, are present in the American city from the Civil War to President Clinton's "race initiative" program in 1997.

11. The capital itself became a contested site and in 1873. "The Congress, in desperation, approved a plan for two capitals." Reps, *The Making of Urban America*, 241.

12. The constitutional amendments attest to the necessary openness of these borders.

13. *Pull* versus *push* refers to the opposition *active* versus *passive* in the reception of the information conveyed by the World Wide Web versus television. It also refers to the absence of advertising, which is forced on the television viewer, which characterized the early stages of the Internet.

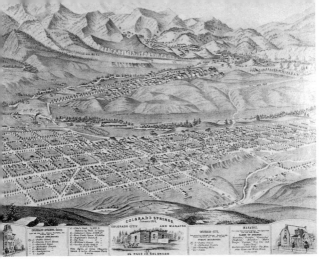

**3.** The centrifugal process of *sprawl* that produces the dissolution of the traditional configuration of the city that in the fantasy is transformed into a garden. The road rather than the buildings and spaces become the urban ordering devices, the totalizing power of the national highway system and its effect, the acceleration of the process that consolidates the suburban city supported in part by nonpaid homeworkers.

**4.** The process of urban *globalization*. Once the territorial city is in place, the distinction urban versus nonurban looses its meaning and is replaced by the opposition real versus virtual. The World Wide Web is the new site where the flows are established and where the new public and private spaces are constructed. The effect on the previous cities is dramatic.

### THE URBAN GRID AND THE ORDER IN THE PLAN

The establishment of an order in the plan of the American city took place in two stages. The first stage involved the projection of the fantasies generated by European architecture (mimesis), and therefore a movement away from the plans of the existing European cities. The insistence of the gridded plan during colonial times, despite the cultural differences among the colonizing efforts (starting with the Spanish, followed by the French and then the English pre-Revolutionary grids) reveal a shared European colonial fantasy of gridded urban plans.[14] The superficial resemblance of the different gridded

plans, perceived as the generic similarity of the colonial plan, obscures the specificity and persistent influence of, for instance, William Penn's plan for Philadelphia or the radical transformation involved in James Oglethorpe's plan for Savannah.

The move of unification represented by the one-mile (or continental) grid that follows the patchwork produced by the earlier colonial interventions can be seen as the second stage in the attempt to define an American gridded plan. The *continental grid*, which structures most of the American territory, is a "post-Revolutionary" and distinctly American plan, proposed by Jefferson and not directly related to any of the "origins" of the gridded urban plan. It should be seen as a step outside this play, as a move towards differentiation, involving a drastic unification and a radical change of scale.

The continental grid represents the simultaneous abandonment of the European models and the *invention* of a new *scale*. The invention was not the grid itself. The first settlement in Ohio where the Commons were planned on the basis of an implied one-mile grid is documented as early as 1765.[15] What was new in the application of the Land Ordinance of 1785 was that the relentless inscription of the grid in the land determined not just the settlement pattern in rural sections but the planning of the future towns themselves. The planning tool and the measuring tool were collapsed in one when the one-mile grid that defined the townships was "stretched" toward the west to the shore of the Pacific. When the American settlers crossed the barrier of the Appalachian

14. Reps mentions three different sources to the grid as an ordering device in the establishment of the American city. First is the Law of Indies, where a simple architectural grid determines the foundation of the Spanish towns well before the first English colonists came to North America. Second, the more complex gridded plans of the French Bastides, and finally the architectural city plans for London after the Great Fire, which represents a third kind of urban

configuration (Reps, *The Making of Urban America*). The first two types of plan still exist and coexist with the dominant English and American plans and while "the Spanish and French gridded plans occupied at first discrete segments of the continent . . . their direct legacy is fairly apparent, if greatly diminished in modern times." Conzen, *The Making of the American Landscape*, introduction.

15. "Another township may be laid out joining this, upon the same plan, and as many more as you please upon the same line without losing any ground." Reps, *The Making of Urban America*, 210.

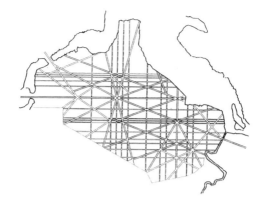

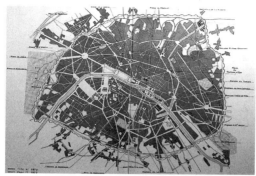

LEFT: View of Colorado Springs, Colorado, 1871

RIGHT: Plan of Washington, D.C.; Haussmann's Paris, c. 1870

Mountains into the Ohio Valley, they left behind the "European city models" brought by the first settlers and the grid became the tool that generated their towns. The colossal grid will become not only the structure of cities such as Chicago, but it will anticipate the scale of the car[16] and therefore the armature of a megacity such as Los Angeles, the "glue" that holds together the gridded cities of "classical" scale, such as Santa Monica, Pasadena, or downtown Los Angeles.[17]

However, when Reps wrote in 1965 that "America lives on a giant gridiron imposed on the natural landscape by the early surveyors carrying out the mandate of the Continental Congress,"[18] he could not foresee the changes that would affect the American city in the next thirty years, although most of the symptoms were already evident. The suburban and X-Urban cities that now cover most of the territory represent the failure of the grid. These new cities have developed with "organic" patterns related to Romantic planning, to the English garden, and to freeway configurations and have been juxtaposed with and sometimes overlapped onto the older grided areas (which were never consistent themselves).

The Cartesian philosophical background that underlies both democracy and the continental grid further undo the notion of an American origin. In fact we are dealing with the American implementation of European philosophical notions. The paradox is explained by the fact that disidentification harbors the identity it seeks to deny: the most American of all grids, the continental grid, comes from Europe. The

same will happen with Washington, D.C., the city representing the Union, which was modeled *in plan* after Versailles. Washington is the ideal city representing the absolutism of imperial power,[19] and in *section* establishes a datum following the example of Paris.[20]

Is this "grid," which from the beginning was the basis of the American city plan — one of the instances of articulation between architecture and the city, or simply a geometric order?

Two different geometries are at work in the grid itself. First, a "metrical geometry" organizes a consistent body of propositions that obtain classic exposition in Euclide's *Elements*, concerned with the ratios and equalities of lines, areas, and angles, a geometry of touch.[21] Second, there is a projective geometry, one more concerned with pictures or maps, a geometry of image. Architecture — a metric organization judged optically — mixes both geometries.[22] While the grid works as an overlay in the survey it acts as an underlay that attempts to exercise a hold on form in architecture. As an overlay, the strict regularity of the *geometric grid* allowed the measured land to exhibit its irregularities.

In fact the *geometric grid* becomes *architectural* at the point where it fails to impose its order; for instance, when the apparatus of architecture acts upon the geometrical grid, when the section is related to the plan, when the building imposes functional limits or when the architect's unconcious disrupts the logic of the grid. The *architectural grid* becomes *urban* when subverted by the fundamental antagonism between architecture and the city. The relationship between these two

16. I was told in the 1980s by a local architect looking at my urban drawings that the highways on the one-mile grid of Los Angeles are the only roads where traffic always flows, even at rush hour.

17. Besides the continental grid, an ever-expanding inventory of gridded urban plans was created after the Revolution, where different notions of grid were articulated to the generation of the urban plan in an open ended play of differences.

18. Reps, *The Making of Urban America*, 217.

19. However this ideal city plan is overlapped onto a gridded plan.

20. "In Paris it is forbidden to build a house beyond a given height." Jefferson draft, "A proclamation," dated 30 March 1791, Saul Padover, *Thomas Jefferson and the National Capital* (Washington, D.C., 1946), quoted by Reps in *The Making of Urban America*.

21. Thomas L. Heath, *Thirteen Books of Euclide's Elements* (New York: Dover, 1956).

22. Robin Evans, *The Projective Cast* (Cambridge, Mass.: The MIT Press, 1995), xxvi, xxxi, and xxxiii. Euclide's geometry still resonates in the contemporary architecture that attempts to disidentity with it but, as we said when referring to the American grid, it harbors the identity it seeks to deny.

RIGHT: Chicago Tribune Building competition entries
by Walter Gropius, Max Taut, Ludwig Hilbersheimer,
and others, 1922

INSET: Chicago Tribune Tower

practices is not only very complex but also enigmatic since the constant attempts to establish the relationship ultimately fail. The transformation of the architectural grid into the *urban grid* is a first step in the always frustrating and frustrated process of establishing this relationship.[23]

The physical city produced by the grid in America is different from the European city, and not defined only by the opposition between scattered versus attached patterns of building. The European city develops through transformations and mutations that deal with the city in terms of the opposition between buildings or urban fabric as *solids* that configure streets and squares as *voids*. The syntax is determined by the extrusion of the plan, by the opposition of center versus edge (the city walls), and by the linear incisions through the fabric that change configuration in the different urban formal regimes (orthogonal streets in the Renaissance or diagonals in the Baroque.) The American city, instead, develops through an order of *objects* sitting in a *field*. The stage of solidity and building contiguity should be seen as a temporary phase due to densification. Since the mid-twentieth century the American city has been visually returning to the cityscape of objects on a field. The syntax given by the two-dimensional field of the grid suggested from the outset a planar strategy. The skyscraper city will take this gridded city as a point of departure and propose a strategy for the section.

23. The lines of the grid that support walls in architecture support spaces in the city. The grids tend to become even, so the center of the grid becomes a street, not a block. Something of the character of the wall remains when the solid becomes void: the American street tends to be a place of division, that separates to different sectors or areas and not a "space" as in the case of the European street.

## THE SKYSCRAPER AND THE FREEDOM
## (AND DISORDER) IN THE SECTION

The process launched by the relentless inscription of the continental grid and the failed American attempts to introject the European urban images continued with the invention of a new urban configuration at the end of the nineteenth century, a second moment in the production of the identity of the American city. The skyscraper, which is considered an American invention, becomes the site for a typological play that represents a radical break with the European extruded fabric and produces a different city. As a major factor in the reversal of the flow between Europe and America, the skyscraper will provide at the symbolic level the basic figure in the construction of the image of the American city as the scene of the future

The skyscraper brings to the vertical dimension what the grid brought to the horizontal: the possibility of infinite extension that is metaphorically present in the name "skyscraper."[24] While the grid brought order and rhythm to the horizontal plane, the skyscraper brings freedom and chance to the vertical dimension by breaking through the datum produced by the constraint of the staircase (the four- to seven-story building characteristic of the European pre-elevator buildings). The skyscraper produces a change in the symbolic economy of high-rise structures: the equivalence between the high-rise and the "monument" (the needle, obelisk, and tower) is now subverted, displaced to the "building," which blurs the opposition building/monument. The skyscraper displaces the architectural conflict between the building (construction) and the monument (the urban ) into the vertical dimension.

The symbolic question proposed by the skyscraper is presented in its anagrammatic structure[25] as a building disseminated in the city that parallels the role played by the column in its relation to the classical building ( the column works as an anagram disseminated in the body of the classical building). The skyscraper is also the place where the grid, which was exclusively present in the urban plan, starts working anagrammatically in the building section.[26]

As with the grid, a similar play of transformation and subversion took place with the skyscraper. Developed between the 1850s and the 1890s, this new type results from a close relationship between technological (elevator), structural (steel structure), and functional innovation (the office building). The problem of configuration proposed by the skyscraper 'was how to articulate the fluid vertical continuum, how to go from the smooth to the striated. The solution was given by the classical tripartite structure of the column, which had already been displaced to the elevation of the classical building. Since the formal restlessness of the building defies the notion of type, the tripartite structure will only provide a point of departure for a process of typological transformation, where the variability of the type escapes the limits of architecture.[27] First come the high-rise building that already poses the questions of typological transformations that the skyscraper is going to develop. The American city is not about typology but about transformations

24. See Agrest, "The Sky's the Limit," in Agrest, *Architecture from Without*.

25. Ibid.

26. Colin Rowe, "Chicago Frame," in *The Mathematics of the Ideal Villa* (Cambridge, Mass.: The MIT Press, 1982).

27. The difference with a classical process of transformation resides in the heterogeneity of the configurations that provide the stable moments of this process coming from different architectural and nonarchitectural languages.

INSET: Chicago Tribune competition entry
by Adolf Loos, 1922

RIGHT: Nineteenth–century American pastoral
fantasy

FAR RIGHT: 1950s suburban scene

affecting its morphology and typology. Examples include the typological transformations of the high-rise Wilshire Boulevard corridor in Los Angeles, the tripartite "high-rise palazzo" structure of Park Avenue in New York, Raymond Hood's blurring of the tripartite Gothic style of the Chicago Tribune building, and the uninterrupted vertical motif of the Daily News building facades in New York.

The skyscraper forces architecture to confront the impossibility of its articulation with the city at the level of the building. The grid becomes architectural and urban when its identity as a neutral field is lost, when its order is lost, when it is subverted. With the skyscraper, the architectural identity is never resolved because of the lack of a specific figural resolution. With the skyscraper, it is easy to fall into eclecticism since anything goes in terms of configuration as opposed to the difficulty or almost the impossibility of transforming the geometric grid into

architecture. The skyscraper's modernity is contradicted by the impossibility of resolving its figure and the persistence of the column in its figural expression.

The skyscraper introduces a new situation in the relationship of identification between Europe and America: Europe identifies with America. At the end of the nineteenth century, while America builds the Columbian Exhibition (celebrating the 500th anniversary of the discovery of America) as a "European" city of cardboard and stucco to fill the lack of a *past*, Europe starts to build visions of an urban *future* of steel and glass. Europe wants to be modern (Adolf Loos and many other European architects come to America to learn from its cities) and the European city wants to be like the American city (Le Corbusier's Ville Contemporaine demonstrates the identification with the American city and its role in the construction of identity in modernist architecture).[28] Simultaneously, with the identification to European architecture embodied in the tripartite structure of the skyscraper, the impulse to differentiate in America will produce an identification with the Gothic, the Other of classical architecture that allows for the transformational play of the type, producing an unstable type in constant flux.[29]

Adolf Loos's project for the Chicago Tribune Building competition preannounces a colossal city in ruins.[30] In fact, the Loos column is the signifier that represents the skyscraper city (as the final chapter of the classical city) for the city to come, a city of objects, the suburban city. Loos's entry to the Chicago Tribune competition sutures the split

28. What about the Cartesian skyscraper as an attempt to produce a domesticated form of the skyscraper? While the antagonism embodied in the skyscraper is domesticated by architecture, and the freedom in section is lost because of extrusion that is the operation of the classical city, Le Corbusier's genius resides in the use of extrusion to defeat the columnar meaning. What about Le Corbusier's Ville Contemporaine? Is it still part of the classical city, or could one say the classical city is part of contemporary city which presents the full picture of the classical city?

29. Agrest, "The Sky's the Limit," in Agrest, *Architecture from Without*.

30. Ibid.

produced by the entrance of this new type — an object that is urban and escapes the urbanity as defined by the European city. It is a lucid theoretical statement on the skyscraper seen as an object of which the column is the formal structure, escaping fabric while sitting on a base made out of fabric.[31]

Although the American grid is not about fabric, and it has distanced itself from the European architectural urban grid (the Renaissance pictorial spaces), it still harbors a possible relationship with the European grid.[32] While the gridded city still implies fabric, the skyscraper city is made out of objects that try to free themselves from the plan, looking for a field that is what the next city will bring to the foreground.

## THE GARDEN WHERE THE CITY WAS BUILT

The first two American urban mutations preserve to a certain extent the image of the European city while a new syntax and a new semantic network is developed. The urban laboratory produced by these two cities is the most limiting for the institutionalized practice of architecture and the most open for an experimental architecture that develops in the margins of the system.

The third American city develops a new pragmatic dimension (in the sense that is not just about the syntactic/semantic urban systems and processes but about the relationship to the subject, in particular to its role as observer)[33] and establishes a new symbolic order. The garden as signifier in the classical system of architecture was the place of

subversion, of the forbidden, the *other* of the building. Its absence in modernism is correlative to its (supposedly) absolute presence: the "contemporary city is built on a garden." In America the garden is a major signifier within a chain that includes the lawn, the green, the national park, and the national highway system (the paths of the continental garden allowing the cars to glide).

The construction of the suburban city implied two stages. In the first stage a move of differentiation with respect to the European city is based on the displacement of its focus from urbanism to landscaping. This displacement produces an uncanny inhabited garden and strange typological transformations due to the relation between the building and the car. In the second stage, a move towards mimesis shrinks the bourgeois garden of the early suburbs and, with the multiplication of the single-family house, creates a new type of scattered fabric where most of the white middle class live.

From the beginning the garden was a key figure in the American Imaginary. The fantasy of America as virgin land, an Edenic garden, exists in colonial times and persists after the Revolution. We call it a fantasy because the Edenic garden is a projection on a territory where there were few geographic areas that had escaped human intervention before the Europeans came to America.[34] It also has, as all fantasies do, the role of screening and supressing a fact. In this particular case the existence of the pre-Columbian cultures that occupied the land for 15,000 years. This suppression will act as a symbolic condition —

31. One of the implications is the impossibility of a generalized objecthood in the European city but also in the architectural Imaginary: when the goal is achieved, architecture is lost. The work of Giovanni Battista Piranesi, in particular the Campus Martius, stands as an exploration of this impossibility.

32. Which is what Luis Cerda produces in his plan for Barcelona of 1854: buildings as extrusions of a gridded plan.

32. Charles Sanders Peirce, *Peirce on Signs: Writings on Semiotic*, James Hoopes, ed. (Chapel Hill: University of North Carolina Press, 1991).

34. Conzen, *The Making of the American Landscape*, 6. This is not to deny the original geographic conditions that existed before the Native American populations occupied the continent.

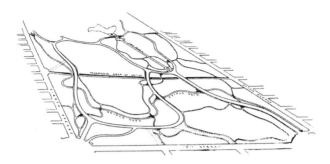

America as a place without a past — for the construction of what was going to be viewed as the scene of the future. America has a past that cannot be erased, a past that altered the environment in fundamental ways, that left indelible traces in the urban discourse (the names) and in the plans (the disturbances of the grid produced by American Indian trails). Finally, it is a fantasy that made possible (in less than 200 years) the fastest transformation ever of a physical environment.[35]

Beginning in Jefferson's time, the cardinal image of American aspirations was a well-ordered green garden magnified to continental size. For more than a century Americans held onto the myth of the garden, not unlike the one that Jefferson had set forth in 1785.[36] Perhaps because, as Alexis de Tocqueville wrote in 1848, "they broke the ties of attachment to their native soil long ago, and have not formed new ones since."[37] The buildings were placed on this "new soil" rather than extruded from it and therefore preserved their objecthood, a behavior that was going to persist in every one of the "American cities" that we described: gridded, skyscraper, suburban, and X-Urban. Also, because of "their restless spirit" and their "extreme love of independence," the autonomy of the building at the basis of the scattered pattern of the suburban city guarantees the dominance of the garden over the city by preventing the cohesiveness given by the European urban fabric.

The American urban discourse developed in two different directions: first, "where nature offered and exemplary form," and second where

nineteenth-century European urban architecture provided the models for civic design.[38] In the nineteenth and early twentieth centuries, the American city was the object of two different types of practice organized by two urban discourses, one of differentiation (introverted, progressive, as in Frederick Law Olmsted), and the other receiving its image from outside (extroverted, conservative, as in Daniel H. Burnham). Progressive American urbanism originates in the European English garden. It is best represented by Olmsted, who had been developing and constructing new urban concepts in relation to the new economic, political, and ideological management techniques. However, here too, the elements that seem to originate in an identification with Europe contain new American strategies that blur and subvert the architectural oppositions: Burnham's extrusions that produce object buildings subverting the extrusion-fabric relationship and also fabric as object that presupposes a field for the fabric to be read as object.

35. Stanley W. Trimble, "Nature's Continent," in Conzen, *The Making of the American Landscape*, 9.

36. Thomas Jefferson, *Notes on the State of Virginia*, edited by William Peden (Chapel Hill: University of North Carolina Press, 1996).

37. Alexis de Tocqueville, *Democracy in America* (New York: Vintage, 1990).

38. M. Christine Boyer, *Dreaming the Rational City* (Cambridge, Mass.: The MIT Press, 1983).

The change of direction of the flow, which started with the sky-scraper, will be established with the garden. The park that covers the ground of Ville Contemporaine, the urban sea of trees, had been an important concept of American planning since the 1850s. Olmsted's Central Park contained ideas (i.e., the separation of streets that are pure circulation, independent of the park) that predate Le Corbusier's Ville Contemporaine. But it is in Prospect Park, Brooklyn, where the park expands into the city through a system of parkways. The park becomes not just a fundamental element in the urban structure but an instrument of planning.[39]

With the suburban city, a new urban configuration emerges, for which the old architectural categories embedded in patterns of opposi-tions going back to the fifteenth century may not be suitable anymore. From the point of view of urban identity, a complete reversal is pro-duced in the relationships between desire/identification and Europe/America: now Europe wants to be like America, and America wants to have the world. It is the beginning of what is going to become a global hegemonic role: first, while the suburban city was being built, as one of the two world powers in the political antagonistic division proposed by the Cold War, and now when the X-Urban city not only develops in America but spreads around the world, as the only superpower in the new "global order."

## THE DISEMBODIED CITY

A fourth fantasy is now in development: the contemporary X-Urban city, the place where the new processes and structures that define the latest stage of global capitalism inscribe this order in the urban realm. Perhaps what triggers the development of the successive cities is desire: every time an object is reached, a new one seems to occupy its place. Once the grid reaches the West Coast, a new object is given; instead of horizontal displacement towards the West, the object of desire is displaced vertically to the sky. However, once the sky is attained the object is displaced from the compact to the scattered, from the exterior to the interior, not just the private put also a multiplicity of public spaces. Now that the city is being both gated and globalized, a new displacement is taking place, from the physical to the virtual dimension promoted by the World Wide Web.

In the end, the urban processes triggered in America by the urban grid, the skyscraper, and the urban garden in the never-ending quest for urban identity confirm the precarious nature of the fixation implied by the establishment of any urban order.[40] The American city stands for the incomplete and open character of urban identity that is never positive and closed in itself, but always constituted as transition, relation, difference.

39. Ibid., 165.

40. I am paraphrasing Ernesto Laclau and Chantal Mouffe, *Hegemony and Socialist Strategy*, 98.

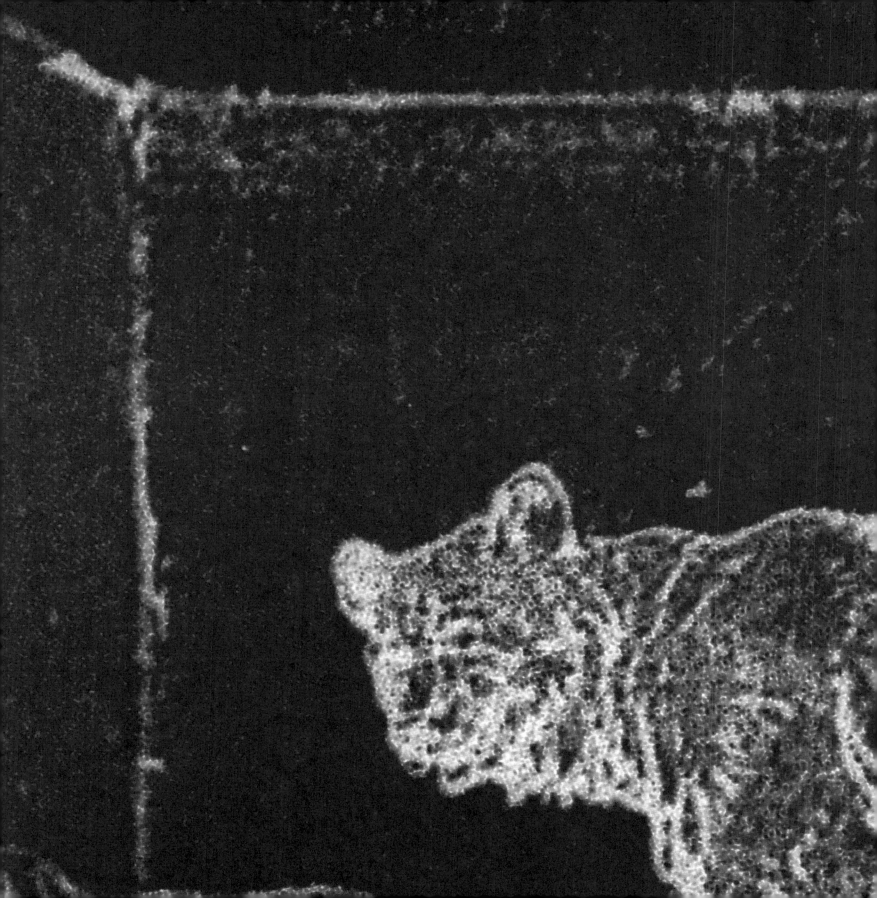

# The City as the Object of Architecture

The fantasies imagined by European modernist urbanism (for example, Le Corbusier's architectural urban fantasy of a city of glass towers on a park, with wide streets on a gridded pattern, where people walk on elevated walkways) depict the impossible relation of architecture to the *object-cause* of its desire, *the city*. The object of the fantasy neither exists in the reality of the city nor can it be literally realized. Why would architects fantasize a totally different city only fifty years after the nineteenth-century rebuilding of the European cities with a totally different strategy — monumental boulevards defined by street walls cut through the medieval fabric? Because the modernist architect's desire was not for the existing city, because more in general, desire is not something given: urban fantasies construct architecture's desire itself by giving its coordinates, by locating its *subject* and specifying its *object*.[1] The construction of desire entails not just depicting a future scene and designating its elements — the garden with objects, the modernist grid, the Cartesian skyscraper — but also designating the gaze that witnesses it. In the case of Le Corbusier, a critical fantasy is directed against the classical city. The gaze comes from the conservative architects and politicians who want to preserve the old European cities as reality and model, cities that, in Le Corbusier's modernists eyes, were crushed by history, stuffed with old buildings with dark interiors and paralyzed by congested streets.

The city has been the object of architectural desire from the moment architectural discourse was established with Alberti's theory: an articulation of two illegible texts, one written, (Vitruvius's *Ten Books on Architecture*) and one built (the Roman ruins).[2] The constitutive moment represented by Alberti takes place at a time when, in Europe, the cities as a political economic structure "come back."[3] It is in this context that architecture is called into being in relation to the city as its *other*. This relationship was established on the basis of a "shared" object, the building, as the object of both practices. In fact, the signifier /building/ collapses two objects — the urban building and the architectural building — as one. The building,[4] as part of the city, is "outside" architecture — it is simply a pile of stones. Beauty and ornament can transform the stones into an architectural building, a transformation that paradoxically requires a separation of the architect from the building, from its site, from its construction.

1. Žižek, *The Sublime Object of Ideology*.

2. This allowed for multiple reinterpretations of the original texts. Pollio Vitruvius, *The Ten Books on Architecture* (reprint, New York: Dover, 1960).

3. Actually the cities have been back since the 1100s. See Benevolo's *The History of the City*.

4. Alberti, *The Ten Books of Architecture*, 156.

The constitutive act establishes a difference, a distance between the architect and the builder, the urban building and the architectural building, that will result in a separation structured as a relation of subordination. From the position of domination, the architect will attempt to close the gap, to attain that which was lost in the differentiation: the building. The lack is sutured by representing what had been excluded in establishing its identity: the work of the carpenter, the construction of the building with the hands instead of the mind. The architectural discourse that becomes an integral part of the practice will register the string of exclusions as the nonmarked terms in an oppositional structure. Where the building, the builder, and the site are represented by discursive "stand-ins," this oppositional structure will split the building into opposing sites (the architect's atelier versus the construction site), the skills into opposing practices (architect versus builder), and the means of production into opposing techniques (design versus building).

Two architectural fantasies concerning the subject and the object designate the elements that could not be integrated in the symbolic structure of architecture. The first is the artistic fantasy where architecture establishes its place as an artistic practice, defining a *creative subject* while occupying the place of the builder: it is a doubling of architecture that wants to be in two places at the same time. The definition of architecture as the "mother" of the other arts obscures the reality of the disturbing in-between that defines architecture as a practice where the architect is neither an autonomous artist, nor a carpenter building for a "client" in the context of the city. Correlated to this subject, this fantasy defines an *object* that also pretends to be in two places at the same time: in the design, which in this fantasy starts from scratch (devised through the architect's own mind and energy), and in the body of the building (realized by construction). The effect of the doubling of the object is the concealment of the the apparatus of representation and of the drawing as the space of architectural production.

The second object-subject fantasy is the urban fantasy: architecture's desire to domesticate the wild economic and political forces that traverse the urban body to impose an order. It is the doubling of architecture that wants to be within its own boundaries and have an effect outside. The architectural-urban fantasy — an architectural universe of buildings in which the city is the largest building — fills out a fundamental lack in architecture, the void left by the loss of the reality of the process of construction and of the building itself. The fantasy implies the reduction of the physical-spatial reality of the city to the status of the architectural building: the city as an object of architectural desire is the city as building.[5] The moment the architectural gaze hits the city, its shapes become the focus, an opening toward a symbolic process that eclipses the actions that take place in it, that shifts the focus from the urban scene where "life" takes place to the stage itself, where real time recedes and space comes to the foreground. However, the reality of the city as a process, as an economic dynamo,[6] a place of both physical and non-physical exchange, has always resisted the suppression of time, of differ-

---

5. ". . . for if a City, according to the Opinion of Philosophers, be no more than a great House, and, on the other Hand, a House be a little City. . . ." Alberti, *Ten Books on Architecture*, 23.

6. Fernand Braudel, *The Structures of Everyday Life: The Limits of the Possible, Civilization and Capitalism: 15th–18th Century*, vol. 1 (Berkeley: University of California Press, 1992), 479.

7. The separation of the two fantasies is a theoretical construction, since they always work in "tandem." The separation makes it possible to perceive the changes in their role in the long duration. For four hundred years the artistic fantasy has a dominant role, and it is only in the last hundred years that the urban fantasy has become dominant. This change is overdeter mined by the speed of urban growth, by the acceleration in the rhythm of urban mutations, and by the reversal of the flows from America to Europe during the last century.

ence, of the contingent, of its reduction to the status of a building; that is, to the spatiality and totalizing nature of the object implied by the architectural urban practice. Nevertheless, while the architectural urban fantasies will never reach their object, they will make possible the triangulation between architecture, the European city and the American city.[7]

## THE OBJECT OF THE URBAN FANTASY

The city has always eluded the architect. It has been attainable neither in space (for instance, when the Renaissance city was projected across the Atlantic), nor in time (when the Baroque city was realized in the late 1800s.)[8] A major obstacle to architecture, which has always been dependent on totalizing notions — the city as building or the city as a network of monuments — is the city's resistance to the notion of a whole. The city presents to architecture an open play of differences within a potentially infinite field of shapes. Since this field resists closure, the city stands as an obstacle to the architectural efforts to domesticate that play, to impose a totalizing order. Another obstacle is presented in architecture itself: it is architecture's resistance to the temporal dimension where the urban processes take place. These processes always overflow the institutionalized framework of the practice of architecture, which, in its pursuit of the city, can approach it but never quite get there. Architecture is too slow or too fast, it rebuilds the past or projects an impossible future,[9] but it can never insert itself into the contingency of the urban present. The movement of the choreography of desire flows from architecture to the city, from the architectural to the nonarchitectural. But desire also flows back from the city (the nonarchitectural) to architecture. It is in this space where the imaginary and symbolic constructions that architecture fantasizes in its pursuit of the city are assembled.

Despite the impossibility of architecture to force a total order upon the urban play, despite the constant failure to realize total order, since the Renaissance, architects have proposed totalizing designs in Europe. Starting with the early architectural treatises such as Antonio Averlino Filarete's *Treatise on Architecture*, these designs have depicted the configuration of entire cities, not just plans but also architectural buildings, a notion that persists until the modernist urbanistic theories. These architectural fantasies are realized in partial and fragmented ways: different degrees and kinds of architectural domestication and sometimes articulations between architecture and the city have taken place in Europe as a result of particular political conjunctures (papal Rome, royal Paris, etc.) that made it possible. While the nonarchitectural urban fantasies in America, the gridded city, the city of skyscrapers, and the suburban city have always been realized, the difficulty of imposing an architectural order beyond the plan has always been enormous.[10] However, the American context paradoxically provides the conditions for one architectural fantasy to be realized and function as the exception: Washington, D.C., the city representing the Union.[11] Washington is the only American city whose identity is defined by repeatedly striving to inscribe a totalizing order. That effort, which is staged apparently as a

8. In implementing some Baroque principles (albeit in a very different historical context), the nineteenth-century capitals produced a city as different form the Baroque as the images produced by photography were from the Renaissance figuration — despite the relationships between the photographic mechanism and perspective. However, the opening of the new Boulevards in Haussmannian Paris perpetuated the fiction of the urban observer of the camera obscura was still viable, in a way paralleling photography's recreation and perpetuation of the subject of perspective.

9. Francoise Choay, *L'urbanisme: utopies et réalités* (Paris: Éd. du Seuil, 1965).

10. The combination of democracy and capitalism produces an extraordinary resistance to any attempt to inscribe an architectural order.

11. Or, perhaps we should say "almost" realized since L'Enfant was fired when he refused to accommodate to various economic-political constraints. See Reps, *The Making of Urban America*, 256.

play of distorting mirrors reflecting the European city,[12] has the role of suturing in the physical reality of the city the successive voids produced: first by the political cut effected by the Revolution, and then by the division and struggle among states that culminates in the Civil War. The unique history of Washington has been determined by a double condition of "otherness": Washington, the "internal other" of the other American cities, is an uncanny refraction of its "external other," the European city.[13]

The resistance that architecture finds in the American city is correlated to the resistance within architecture to consider the American city in architectural terms. For hundreds of years, since Alberti, the architects had gone to Rome, not just to measure the buildings themselves, but to expose the subject of architecture to the gaze of the ruins, of the built text that constituted the practice. The American city, as opposed to Rome, was beyond the architectural field of vision, not just because it was considered an inferior version of the European city, but also because of what was considered the deficient configuration of its gridded plan. This resistance weakens when the European architects are subject of the gaze of the American city in the late nineteenth and early twentieth century; that is, the gaze of the modern city, the gaze coming from the future. The effect of this "evil eye" is ultimately devastating for the architectural status quo: a violent reaction takes place against classical architecture and a new architectural universe is invented.

While the architectural gaze produces in some instances urban restructurings (that ultimately never coincide with the architects desire), the urban gaze produces traumatic effects on architecture. In looking back at "architecture from without," the city interpellates architecture, inducing sometimes pathological urban fantasies. Pope Sixtus V's Rome, Bernini's St. Peter's Square, Piranesi's readings of Rome, Ledoux's ideal city, and Le Corbusier's Ville Contemporaine are not part of the "normal" discourse of architecture, but are symptomatically excessive, out of place with respect to their discursive contexts.[14] Why? Because of the constitutive role of the city in the establishment of the architectural practice, and the traumatic effect of any attempt to "reintroduce it" into architecture. Because of the historical failure in this repression of the city, which has both been contained outside architecture and represented inside architecture through urban fantasies.

The traumatic effects of the radical changes that take place in the early twentieth century are overdetermined by confrontation with new challenges due to the reversal in the direction of flows in the historical triangular relationship between architecture, the European city, and the American city. With the opening to the American city comes the challenge for architecture proposed by the introduction of the skyscraper, a building type that deals with the extremely high density but that also questions both the traditional city of fabric, the traditional scene where architecture was always staged, and the notion of type itself, which in the nineteenth century came to occupy a prominent role in architectural

---

12. In doing so, Washington also strove to transform an order that was initially conceived as a physical setting for autocratic forms of government.

13. This doubling repeats at every level. Washington's own history starts with a split caused by the disagreement over its location (North versus South) and the compromise that consolidates a single capital. The survey of the new district was commissioned to Andrew Ellicott and Major Pierre Charles L'Enfant

(whose father was a court painter in Versailles) was commissioned first to draw the ground and the plan of the city. The structure of the plan overlapped two different strategies: "a regular distribution with every street at right angles ... and diagonal avenues to and from every principal place ... giving them reciprocity of sight and by making them thus seemingly connected."

14. In turn, as we have seen, these fantasies are introjected back by the city that is constantly restructured; in Baroque Rome when the entire city rather than the Church became a sacred space, in the Enlightenment when a new political-economic order was institutionalized, at the beginning of the twentieth century when the pressures of the industrial city forced the restructuring of the old urban structures, and now again with the radical restructuring brought by the global informational city.

theory and practice. The challenge presented to architecture by the American city provokes and produces the urban mutation introduced by the radical European modernist fantasies.

While the previous fantasies were rereadings of the Roman and Greek cities of the past — and the Baroque reaction against these readings — the new fantasies look at the scene of the future, the American city. However, they do not see the city of skyscrapers: the urban fantasy functions now as a screen that not only hides the antagonisms in the relation between architecture and the city, but keeps the American city out of sight, or located in a blind spot.

## THE SUBJECT OF THE URBAN FANTASY

Correlated to its *object* (the city), the urban fantasy provides the location of a *subject*, not very different from the "creative subject" of the artistic fantasy.[15] This subject is blind to the reality of a city always already present, the result of accretion, of the overlapping of successive traces on a ground that retains them, a city that resists the notion of starting from scratch, of being constructed by architectural fantasies on a blank piece of paper as a fact that has not yet been built, a city that resists being considered an architectural building. The creative subject of the urban fantasy inhabits a scene of *production* that is almost fully occupied by a multiplicity of economic and political actors, of practices other than architecture, and fails to recognize another possible location for the construction of the urban fantasy scene — the space of reception.[16]

The displacement to the space of reception will take place at a point when the traumatic urban restructuring in postwar Europe and America produces a break, a discontinuity, in the relatively stable structures that organize the recognition of the city. The cities produced by the suburbanization of the American city and the postwar European reconstruction are illegible, an illegibility that particularly concerns the architect. The confrontation with the new city that emerges in the late 1950s and early 1960s results in a theoretical production that accomplishes a critical shift in the position of the architectural subject, from production to reception, from writing to reading.[17] This displacement will produce a major break in the mid-1960s with respect to 1920s modernist architecture's failed attempt to produce a city by locating itself in the traditional site of production.

Reading the city presupposes a subject that is defined by a particular "quilting"[18] that fixates the meaning of the multiplicity of urban signifiers. The illegibility of the new city raises the need to "quilt" the new and old floating signifiers, to fix their meaning, making the city legible again by introducing a *major signifier* to structure the signifying field. This quilting was attempted no just by architects but by various observers who worked in the field of the social sciences and found their object of study in the city, including behavioral scientists, sociologists, and planners; for instance, the disoriented subject and the question of *legibility* in Kevin Lynch,[19] the disembodied exurbanite and the question of *nonplace* produced by the new electronic technology in Melvin Webber,[20]

15. Modernist architecture's notion of *objet type* starts to weaken the creative subject with the idea of an anonymous collective subject. But perhaps as important as that is the idea of an autonomy of architectural form, of an architectural signifier that locates the architect as its subject, as determined by it and not determining it; in other terms, the site of production becomes reduced and passive.

16. While the space of reading was always integral to the dimension of architectural competence it was always seen as subordinated to writing since Alberti. The new situation produces not just a reversal of this position but also, as we will discuss, the blurring of the difference between production and reception.

17. See Aldo Rossi, *The Architecture of the City* (Cambridge, Mass.: The MIT Press, 1982) and Robert Venturi, *Complexity and Contradiction in Architecture*.

18. I refer to Žižek's idea of quilting, which states that by sewing urban configurations and meanings, the structured system of oppositions that make the city understandable and recognizable are produced (i.e., streets/squares; monuments/fabric; attached structures/detached structures; low-rise buildings/high-rise buildings; public buildings/private buildings; etc.). See Žižek, *The Sublime Object of Ideology*.

19. Lynch, *The Image of the City*.

the passive audience of a *spectacular* society in Guy Debord,[21] and the prearchitectural (structuralist) *urban reader* by Michel de Certeau.[22] What these different quiltings have in common is that they ignore and/or suppress the architectural view of the city, and the questions of *form* and *visual enjoyment* of the city, the flow that relates the nonarchitectural city to architecture.

Particularly relevant to our discussion is Kevin Lynch's 1960 text, *The Image of the City*, because his object of study seems to overlap with the architectural object. The urban buildings and spaces addressed by Lynch at a point in history where urban renewal destroys the center city are "innocent" — they have not yet been *hit* by the architectural gaze, they are part of "reality," a stage where "life" and social actions take place.[23] The question addressed by Lynch is the "clarity and legibility of the cityscape,"[24] the ease with which its parts can be recognized and organized into a coherent pattern to provide clues to orientation.[25] Lynch's desire, at a time where the centered city is mutating into something else, the center erased and the suburban city "taking over" the previous city, is not to know and enjoy the form of the city, but to know how to recognize and use the form of the city.[26] Lynch's city is primarily a communicational device, a "transitive" artifact intended to provide directions, to point toward a destination.[27]

Lynch's functionalist view constructs a city as a place of known trajectories, where the illegibility and the resulting opacity created by the restructuring of the city give way to a transparent city. Paradoxically,

when the totally clear and legible city becomes a transitive and neutral vessel for conveying information, we no longer see the city, in the same way that language becomes *invisible* when we are using it (as opposed to the *opaque* language of poetry, where language itself is the focus). Architecture is also interested in making the city "visible" and has therefore introduced *opacity* in the city throughout history, a gesture that was magnified by modernist architecture. However, this was an opacity that presupposed a legible, transparent, and therefore invisible prearchitectural city. So what is to be done when, for the first time in urban history, this "natural"/prearchitectural city becomes opaque, as in the case of Europe and in America in the 1960s? As opposed to the shocking "newness" of modern architecture vis-à-vis the classical city (which brings opacity to the level of *expression*), the postmodernist architects of the mid-1960s produce an "uncanny homeliness" and therefore opacity at the level of *content*.[28] This major restructuring of the theory and practice of architecture is produced by the displacement in architectural production from designing and "writing" a new city to reading a "ready-made" city, and by a correlated displacement of the architect from the traditional position of *creative agent* to the new position of *architectural observer* who rewrites the existing city. Aldo Rossi in Europe and Denise Scott Brown and Robert Venturi in America produce this displacement.[29]

Rossi's *Architecture of the City* presents a theory involving the persistence of form, the insistence of urban traces in the permanent process of

20. Melvin M. Webber, *Urban Place and Nonplace Urban Realm, in Explorations into Urban Structure* (Philadelphia: University of Pennsylvania Press, 1964).

21. Guy Debord, *La societe du spectacle* (Paris: Editions Buchet-Chastel, 1967).

22. Certeau, *The Practice of Everyday Life*.

23. Kevin Lynch's "settlement form" is the spatial arrangement of persons doing things, the resulting spatial flows of persons, goods and information and the physical features which modify space in some way significant to those actions. Lynch, *The Image of the City*, 48.

24. The metaphor of the urban landscape invoked by the term "cityscape" produces the sense of an architectural connection. See Lynch, *The Image of the City*.

25. "A *legible* city would be one whose districts or landmarks of pathways are easily *identifiable* and are easily groped into an overall pattern." The problem being the construction of orientational organizations within the visual chaos of the modern city by means of the reduction of the city to the same five elements that "describe" their image: path, edge, district, node, landmark. See Lynch, *The Image of the City*.

differentiation that characterizes the historical city.[30] Rossi proposes a displacement in the location of the architectural subject of the architectural fantasy, switching its traditional location from the place of production to the place of reception, from writing to reading. When the city and the architectural building are seen in terms of production, "one is the product *of the public*, the other one is *for the public*"[31] and therefore the only place available in the city for the architect is the place of the viewer. What allows this change of location is the extension of the architectural notion of type to nonarchitectural buildings to the fabric of the city. By doing this, Rossi subverts the constitutive distinction between architectural building and urban building, which is "brought into" architecture. What allows this to happen is the notion of analogy, which in Rossi's theory occupies a prominent place. The effect of the analogical mechanism is a displacement of forms, objects, and urban buildings that subvert the humanist notion of scale and the boundaries of architecture itself, opening its lexicon to include the city and the world of ordinary objects.[32] Rossi's notion of permanence in the long duration of the constantly changing city, a reading in which he articulates the city to the Ferdinand de Saussure's notion of langue,[33] allows him metonymically to place architecture in the space of writing.

In America, Venturi and Scott Brown perform a similar operation of displacement of the architectural observer by reading the urban sprawl produced by the suburban city. In a strategic move they align themselves with the vanguard culture of the 1950s and early 1960s.

Particularly, they align themselves with pop art (especially painting), subverting the boundaries of architecture, erasing the distinction between high (architecture) and low (sprawl); that is, proposing an equality and interchangeability of architectural and nonarchitectural shapes. In *Learning from Las Vegas*, Venturi and Scott Brown radicalize Venturi's position in *Complexity and Contradiction in Architecture* by focusing on the new cityscape that results from the suburban mutation, instead of on the permanent elements of the city. While Rossi's concept of permanence alludes to the structural resistance to urban amnesia, the Venturi/Scott Brown reading refers to the resistance of architecture to the new observer, an observer that breaks away from the traditional ambulatory subject to produce a reading in motion (from the car) of a city of signs and the architectural resistance to the new configurations, both lexical and syntactic, produced by urban sprawl.

With Rossi and Venturi/Scott Brown, architecture is drastically restructured and the object of architectural desire is displaced. What the architect desires in the mid-1960s is not just the repertory of configurations and shapes given by a totalizing architectural urban fantasy. The desire now is to produce the articulation of the temporal *diachronic axis of architecture* — the closed space of architectural competence that stands as a challenge to the "formal disorder" of the city, architecture as "high art" — to the *synchronic axis of the city*, the cultural dimension that includes today the "low art" of the urban building, of the developer, and of mass culture, which challenges and opens up the limits of the

26. The social sciences could help one recognize certain trajectories, to facilitate the flow of movement throughout the city.

27. The image of the city is a prestructuralist readings that presupposes an inherent meaning carried by signs defined by a one to one relationship between signifier and signified.

28. These architects obviously produce opacity for the architectural reader at the level of expression since they introduce non-architectural configurations as if

they belonged to the architectural "lexicon." I am using expression and content as in Louis Hjelmslev's model of the sign. See Louis Hjelmslev, *Prolegomena to a Theory of Language* (Madison: University of Wisconsin Press, 1961).

29. Rossi and Scott Brown/Venturi reflect in their work what Jacques Derrida called the "anxiety about language and the question of the sign" that characterized the 1960s. Derrida refers in particular to French structuralism and in general to "thought in all its

domains." Jacques Derrida, "Force and Signification," in Jacques Derrida, *Writing and Difference* (Chicago: University of Chicago Press, 1980), 3.

30. One could say that, in an indirect way, the architecture of the city is a radical approach to the question of the European city through a reading of the American city. The original version and its translations in Europe ignore the question. However, with his English translation, Rossi acknowledges the book as an effect of the gaze of the American city.

architectural. This desire was present since Alberti, when he described the architect as someone who needs to master not only specific architectural knowledge but knowledge of various cultural practices. The impossibility of realizing this desire for an articulation between architecture and the other cultural practices — for a "balance" between them, because of different specificities and historical developments, and ultimately the antagonism between the two axes, the fact that the articulation will always ultimately fail — sustains the city as an object of desire. The *diachronic axis* is the space where historical returns take place even when they appear as a break.[34] The postmodernist articulation that takes place in the 1960s with Rossi and Venturi/Scott Brown produces a historical return that does not necessarily imply a literal repetition, but rather the establishment of the ground where "formal invention is redeployed, where social meaning is resignified, and where cultural capital is reinvested."[35] While attempting to articulate itself to the urban field, architecture produces and develops new forms, not just the known forms of its own "local" architectural forms, but also marginal forms by which dominant forms are resisted and/or subverted.[36]

## ARCHITECTURAL READINGS OF THE URBAN TEXT

The X-Urban mutation of the American city in the 1980s and 1990s presents new difficulties for the articulation of architecture and the city. But it also opens new opportunities, and not just for a *relationship* between the city and architecture where the city remains unchanged while architecture changes itself in an attempt to celebrate the X-Urban city paralleling Venturi's celebration of the suburban city. The present urban conjuncture also presents opportunities for an *articulation*, that is, for the development of a politically resistant form of urban architecture that transforms itself while it questions — and transforms — the status quo of a system committed solely to profit.

The strategy presented here points in that direction. It attempts to "radicalize" the restructuring of architecture accomplished in the 1960s, in particular the reading of the city, not just by looking away to the nonarchitectural urban buildings but by displacing the gaze to the *plan*, by opening up a process of relative autonomy as an investigation of alternative spaces of intervention and the production of alternative configurations. This process actively changes the way we read the city into a first moment in an effort to change the city. This is a *process that opens up the play of form* frozen by both the global city of capital and an architecture inhibited by the enormous weight of modernist architecture, a *play of form* where *form* is not just the perceived shape of the city's physical configuration but a *textual construction* (visual-discursive).[37]

The textual metaphor opens up new questions about the city, architecture, and the problematic of their articulation.[38] What is the *city* if it can be represented by a *text*? And what kind of *text* is the *city*? The textual metaphor opens up the question of the city as memory (of its people), that is, the city as inscription of both permanent traces and the possibility of their erasure. The city not just as another form of writing

---

31. There is a strong connection between the reader of the architecture of the city in Rossi and the surrealist conception of the artist as an "agonized witness" (André Bréton in *Nadja* [New York: Grove Press, 1988]), and the "surprised viewer" (Giorgio de Chirico in *Meditations of a Painter*). See Hal Foster's reading of surrealism in *Compulsive Beauty* (Cambridge, Mass: The MIT Press, 1993). Emphasis mine.

32. It also cancels the notion of scale, and therefore a number of rules of appropriateness.

33. The nonmotivated relationship between form and function which becomes obvious in the long duration of the "urban facts" as opposed to architecture where the short duration provides the illusion of motivation.

34. We have to remember that a historical return was constitutive of the practice of architecture itself.

35. Foster, *Compulsive Beauty*.

36. The articulation of Piranesi's Campus Martius where the urban forces subvert architectural form, with Foley Square in Manhattan, or Le Corbusier's linear projects for Latin American cities of the late 1920s, or Wilshire Boulevard in Los Angeles as examples of this strategy.

37. Gandelsonas, *The Urban Text*.

(writing itself being a supplement to memory) or as a supplement to other cultural texts but more specifically as a *writing mechanism*, similar to the *mystical pad*,[39] the topographic model that Freud constructed as an articulation of writing and the unconscious. The displacement of this "topographic" model to the urban text, allows to account for the simultaneous and contradictory requirements of permanence and erasure that characterize the city. What justifies this displacement is that, at one level, we are dealing in the city with buildings and spaces that are always open to changes, with a level that has an unlimited capacity to transform. At another level, we are also dealing with the urban plan, which can be seen as the ground where the traces are inscribed and indefinitely retained while everything else changes.[40] But there is also a third level, one of social and cultural forces, of practices and institutions that reconciles the other two, that makes possible the realization of the individual building on the collective ground, the transformation of time into space, of history into geography. The city as the object of architectural desire is the one that embodies the two contradictory levels and their possible reconciliation.[41] There is no place for architecture either in the city of memory (which would be a dead city, a museum, a tableau, and where articulation is not possible), or in the city of constant change where nothing remains. In fact these extremes designate the limits of the different conditions imposed by the "writing surfaces" of different cities: while the European city is less erasable at the level of buildings, it has undergone major changes in its plan, which is supposed to be the most resistant to change; the American city's buildings have been deleted many times in the long duration, while its plan resists change. *It is in the space where these two levels are reconciled where architecture finds the site for its articulation with the city, the site where architecture can produce changes that inscribe permanent traces in the urban realm.*

While the city presents different layers of inscription, architecture adds levels of meaning to the city with its own *reading mechanism*. The urban *writing mechanism* offers a text where a wide range of architectural reading strategies "find" or, rather, build their object. Transcription and erasure are the two limits that determine a range of rewriting that begins with the reproduction of the text (historical preservation) and ends with its deletion (tabula rasa). These two extremes are the boundaries where a multiplicity of strategies and tactics define the reading mechanism.[42] This strange confrontation of *architecture's reading* with *urban writing* generates the *space of articulation*, a space where the city resists architecture's desire to transform it and where architecture insists on its transformation. This very book represents another iteration of this insistence.[43]

The architectural reading mechanism is a historical construction, constantly restructured by different optical regimes. It is first described by Alberti as "standing in front of the building" as a mathematics of imaginary additions and subtractions but also transformations, which at that point in history do not distinguish the difference between the reality of the *building* from its *representation*.[44] A different notion of

---

38. Besides opening up questions, the textual metaphor, like all metaphors, closes the discourse by orienting it and fixing the "results" of the investigation. In this case, the textual metaphor has a strategic role in our pursuit of the articulation of the city and architecture, since it leads to the question of reading and to our tactical mode of reading the city (the urban drawings).

39. Jaques Derrida, "Freud and the Scene of Writing," in *Writing and Difference*, 199.

40. The monument, which "represents" as a building the immutability of the plan, has been traditionally the preferred site for the articulation of a writerly architecture and the city.

41. The city, as the object of architecture, is always a rewriting of a previous city.

42. This multiplicity resonates with the dimensions of permanence and change that define the urban writing mechanism.

reading is at work in Andrea Palladio's *Four Books of Architecture*.[45] With this publication of his designs (as opposed to the representation of the buildings), Palladio shows the effect of the optical regime instated by the camera obscura that separates the *building* and its *projection*.[46] The same effect is evident in Giovanni Battista Piranesi's fictional drawings for the Campo Martius where not only the difference between drawing and building but also the *autonomy* of drawing is reaffirmed. With twentieth-century modernism, and in particular with Le Corbusier, the identification of *perception* and *object* ends and perception itself becomes the object of the reading mechanism. According to Le Corbusier, architecture should only be concerned with that which is accessible to the eye. The reading mechanism constructs its object as a systematic structure of oppositions that organizes movement in a sequence propelled by the perception of foreground versus background, shadows versus light, vertical versus horizontal, and so forth.[47]

What is the object of the reading mechanism at work in the urban drawings presented in this text? The question of *desire*, that is, the question of the "urban unconscious" in the process of *articulation of architecture and the city*. The process of reading that breaks away from the modernist perceptual model, still pervasive and determinant in most contemporary readings, takes place in two levels. The first level is accessed through a *differential analysis* based on the plan, which is seen as part of the architectural apparatus.[48] This view of the urban plan radicalizes the timid modernist extrusion of the *urban* plan as opposed to the modernists' view of the *architectural* plan as a battlefield where the antagonism between "pre-existent ideas" and the "*intention motrice*" is deployed and fought. The plan is approached with a multiplicity of reading strategies that range from architectural *determination* implied by the modernist notion of "the plan as generator" to the pure *contingency* embodied in the American city, where the plan plays with or against the architectural sections that rewrite it.

In this first level of reading, the *plan* — a two-dimensional section through the city seen as solids and voids that eliminates the familiar images of the vertical dimension and their sequential perception in time — is *framed* by the reading mechanism providing the entry into the urban text, cutting through, fracturing the unlimited perceptual surface of the X-urban city. How is the *frame* established? By gravitating towards the areas of "scriptural density," the areas of the urban field that present the maximum intensity of tension between permanence and change, where two or more layers of rewriting have left indelible traces. Within this frame, the analytical drawings emphasize graphically the elements of the plan that deviate from the *neutral grid*. For instance, they fragment (New York) and delayer the plan (Boston) and the fabric (New Haven) to depict the modes of coexistence or multiple gridded and non-gridded configurations (Des Moines). They examine the discontinuities in the grid (Atlantic City). They reintroduce and delaminate the grid it in its constituent directions (Chicago). The vertical dimension given by

43. The confrontation usually fails to produce an articulation. For instance, while the eighteenth-century urban drawings had an important internal role in the practice of architecture, in their subversion of the language and the restructuring of the practice as a response to the new city of nineteenth-century capitalism, they did not have an immediate effect on that city. In a symmetrical way, while the nineteenth-century drawings had an important role, external to the practice of architecture in the restructuring of the European capitals, they represent the conservative aspects of architecture compared to the contemporary architectural work produced not just by architects but by engineers who investigated the potential of new technologies and programs.

44. ". . . when we face some other person's building, we immediately look over and compare the individual dimensions, and to the best of our ability consider what might be taken away, added or altered. . . ." Leon Battista Alberti, *On the Art of Building in Ten Books*, (reprint, Cambridge, Mass.: The MIT Press, 1988), 4.

45. Andrea Palladio, *Four Books of Architecture* (reprint, New York: Dover, 1965).

46. However, the commentaries reveal that the attention of the mechanism is placed on the actors and their actions and not in the configuration of the architectural stage.

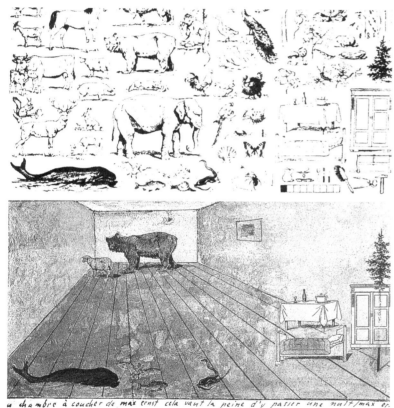

*la chambre à coucher de max ernst cela vaut la peine d'y passer une nuit/max er.*

the buildings complements and/or supplements this analysis in the cases where it plays a significant role,[49] for instance in the representation of the typological transformations of Wilshire Boulevard (Los Angeles).

The reading of the *second level* is guided by a *floating attention*. Here, as opposed to the first level, the reading drifts and proceeds without knowing, retroactively determining the definition of the frame.[50] This framed plan as a *field* of events, mobilizes a "half desire" of the order of "liking and not a 'full desire' of the order of loving" mobilized by the *symptom*.[51] *Symptoms* appear as disturbances of the plan (the anomalies that disrupt the order) and the discourse (they cannot be labeled within architectural discourse, they need to be named). Whereas the construction of the first level presupposes a conscious investment in the field, the symptoms that punctuate the field rise toward us to enter our unconscious. The urban drawings result from this symptomatic reading where the architect's gaze confronts the failures, the "lapsus" of the urban text,[52] which undermine the surface of the first level lifting the architectural boundaries that block the access to other readings.[53] Taking the plan as a point of departure for the urban drawings as ready-made, establishes a link with the operations developed by Max Ernst in what critic Rosalind Krauss calls his "overpaintings." In particular, in Ernst's *Master Bedroom*, "the mechanism of the Mystic writing pad finds its analog in the underlying sheet of the (*ready-made*) teaching aid page . . . while the top sheet appears in the perspectival covering produced by the gouache overpainting."[54] In the

47. The description of the house of the Casa del Noce in Pompeii shows the modernist mechanism at work. Le Corbusier wrote: "Again the little vestibule which frees your mind from the street. And then you are in the atrium; four columns in the middle (four cylinders) . . . but at the far end is the brilliance of the garden seen through the peristyle which spreads out this light with a large gesture. . . . Between the two is the tablinum, contracting this vision like the lens of the camera. On the right and on the left two patches of shade. . . . You have entered the house of a Roman." Le Corbusier, *Towards a New Architecture* (New York: Dover, 1986, a reproduction of the 1931 English translation of the thirteenth French edition), 169–70. The text is organized symbolically by a sequence of interrelated oppositions: small/large, private/public, horizontal/vertical, light/shadow, front/back, interior/exterior, etc.

48. The plan interpellates us, in a similar way as the "ready-made" was selected by attracting the artist attention.

49. The drawings do not always provide a "realist" representation of solids and voids. In fact, most times they represent solids as voids and voids as solids.

urban drawings the underlying sheet is the urban plan and instead of an overpainting, a process of deletion — manual or electronic, as in the Chicago and Des Moines computer drawings — deliminates the plan to create layers that can be overlapped in different combinations to produce sequences of drawings. The drawings are written as a dialogue between two discourses, the ready-made plan that acts as a background against which the architectural writing is inscribed. The floating attention fluctuates between depiction and rewriting (or writing subordinated to reading, or reading as writing), blurring their differences. It is a process where architecture *and* the city occupy and switch the positions of analyst and analysand (the one who is being analyzed), an alternation where each practice traverses the "other"· discursive surface, where architecture traverses the urban discourse, where the city traverses the architectural discourse.

## REWRITING THE CITY

The will to rewrite the city is not the architectural desire to write the city — it is the only way out of desire.[55] It is the way out of the closure defined by the historical relationship between architecture and the city, a closure represented today in the opposition between avant-gardism and traditionalism, between the apolitical architectural commitment to object-fetishism and the hopelessness of an urbanism that clings to the past as a way to obstruct the future.[56] "It is both about freedom" (the possibility of inventing a new articulation between city and architec-

ture) "and about duty"[57] (the necessity of traversing the city if we are to deal with its historical suppression through architectural fantasy) and not about the affectivity of desire.[58]

The displacement to the scene of reading as the starting moment for the process of architectural rewriting — where reading the city is not aimed at an accurate representation but at starting the process of forging a new city — opens up new questions about the scene of writing, about its historical location, about the need to build a new site. The first architectural urban site in the American city is the foundation plans, an ever-expanding reservoir of urban configurations, originally modeled by the Europeans after architectural plans for the colonial city. The second site, at the beginning of the twentieth century, is the city plan that aims to restructure and/or to regulate urban growth. In this second moment that culminates with the City Beautiful movement from the Burnham Plan of Chicago (1908) to the New York Regional Plan (1929), the initiative comes from architecture, which aggressively attempts and partially succeeds to restructure the city. The third moment represents the starting point for the continuing shrinking of the site. The reaction of the planners in the 1950s against the consideration of the city as an architectural object and their emphasis on process radically alters the situation concerning the stage and the actors. In the name of "process," activities are seen as the dominant urban force that denies the relative autonomy of configuration and the possibility of an articulation architecture-city, closing the stage to architecture and opening it

50. We only recognize the logic at work in the definition of the frame when we read the second level.

51. Roland Barthes, *Camera Lucida: Reflections on Photography* (New York: Noonday Press, 1982), 27.

52. "How to read: watch out for the breaks in continuity, for the frontier zones. Be alert to the moment when the shapes change . . . be on the lookout for divergences, contrasts, breaks, frontiers." Braudel,

*The Identity of France*, 51. These incidents are the expression of the residual force of the city that cannot be silenced by the geometry of the grid.

53. Where do these failures take place? In the margins where the grids collide and within the grid, when it encounters the force of previous inscriptions (history and geography) that cannot be completely obliterated by the grid.

54. Krauss, *The Optical Unconscious*, 57.

55. It is perhaps "a way out that can only be aimed at, without the certainty that it is outside the affectivity of desire," Derrida, "Force and Signification" in *Writing and Difference*.

56. I am refering to the projects that take a cultural and formal tabula rasa as a "plane" of departure as well as to the "New Urbanism" represented by Seaside and similar projects including Disney's Celebration.

up to economic-political planning. The spectatorial position taken by architects (as approving or critical spectators) who abandon the active urban interventions that characterized the previous period overdetermines the lack of impact of their projects.

To build a new architectural site in the X-Urban city, a change will be necessary in the space now occupied by the Master Plan, the legal instrument that deals with the long term functional and physical processes that determine the configuration of a town or a city. The Master Plan's role is to regulate those processes but also to fill a void, to mask the absence of architecture.[59] The shapes determined by its regulations (which are answers to social/economic/political questions), in the place of architecture, render the void invisible and obscure the fact that architectural form is absent.

From the initial moment when decisions about urban configuration take place, the displacement of the Master Plan opens up a space where architecture could play an active role in its engagement with the X-Urban city. The Des Moines Vision Plan, for example, represents a possible strategy for building a site in this space.[60] This Vision Plan designates a process of reading and rewriting that abandons the traditional discourse and practice of urbanism, the scale of the architectural building object, its formal and symbolic strategies, the principles of unity, continuity and homogeneity, and begins the construction of a new imaginary where the cultural/aesthetic implications of urban form are articulated to the contemporary restructuring processes of the global city.[61]

Every one of the sites — the gridded foundation plan, the City Beautiful movement, the planner's notion of process as a critique and the city conceived as an object — provided new opportunities that widened the possibilities for an articulation with architecture and expanded the urban play in multiple and even conflicting directions. The site built in the scene of reading confronts a past as a source of "suggestions of how to make the future different."[62] The reading of the city implies not preservation and protection but rewriting as "discord to be resolved in previously unheard harmonies."[63]

57. Derrida, "Force and Signification" in *Writing and Difference*.

58. This decision to rewrite the city is also different from the urban rewriting that is, the economic-political mechanism at work in the urban processes where every city rewrites the previous one.

59. Mario Gandelsonas, "The Master Plan as a Political Site," *Assemblage* 27 (Cambridge, Mass.: The MIT Press, 1996).

60. See "The Des Moines Vision Plan" in Agrest and Gandelsonas, *Works*.

61. Why would cities open up to architecture? At a cultural level, because of the increasing search for local urban identity (as a counterbalance to globalization); at the economic level because the visual configuration of the city is becoming an asset in their competition to attract tourism, at a political level because of the possibilities of consensus related to a local sense of pride. The relationship between drawings, identity construction, and tourism provides a strong argument for the restructuring of the notion of Master Plan incorporating a first moment of Vision Planning that provides the formal conditions for the radical rewriting of the city.

62. Richard Rorty, *Achieving Our Country* (Cambridge, Mass.: Harvard University Press, 1998).

63. Ibid.

# Drawing the American City

In the essay "Architectural Projection," Robin Evans describes projections as "organized arrays of imaginary straight lines that pass through the drawings to corresponding parts of the thing represented in the drawing." "Projection," Evans says, "has become thoroughly directional because of the availability of certain instruments and machines for making pictures; but there is nothing in projection itself to suggest directionality." Projection can work both ways: "architecture provides an instance of the opposite tendency, taking information from flat representations to create embodied objects."[1] However, architecture is not just an active *remodeling* of reality — it also produces *portrayals* when it functions in a reading mode as opposed to its traditional *writing* mode. For hundreds of years the architect was supposed to go to Rome to draw and measure *from* the classical buildings, that is, to "read" the classical buildings. However, he was not supposed to draw the existing city that was seen as the result of contingency as opposed to the order embodied in the buildings. The void produced by the suppression of the city was filled with the drawings that represented projects for ideal cities and urban spaces. Some of these projects were inserted in the reality of this city through the violent destruction of the existing fabric, a practice that grows at an accelerated pace during the nineteenth century.

This representational relationship was not established with the American city until the end of the nineteenth century, when the directionality of the flows between Europe and America was reversed. As we have seen, the "young" American city was considered inferior to the European city, a result of pragmatic forces, sitting on a relentless and meaningless gridded field. At the turn of the twentieth century, when urban drawings are produced in America, they lead to "temporary cities" or *built* fantasies such as the 1892 Colombian Exhibition in Chicago, or to *unbuilt* fantasies such as the 1908 Burnham plan for Chicago.

The void created by the absence of the American city in the architectural discourse was filled with (justified in terms of the dominance of) the neutral and therefore architecturally meaningless grid, as opposed to the perceived contingency that characterizes the elevation of the American city (i.e., the New York skyline). Despite the fact that the resistance to the American city diminishes in the twentieth century, the view of the American city as a nonarchitectural fact is maintained and even reinforced by both its explicit detractors and apparent supporters, by Camilo Sitte, who criticized the modern gridded plans, and by

1. Robin Evans, *Architecture and its Image: Four Centuries of Architectural Representation* (Montréal: Canadian Centre for Architecture, 1989).

Le Corbusier, who qualified the "disorder" of the skyscrapers and the corridor streets they produced as a catastrophe,[2] and who praised a *neutral gridded plan* that did not exist.

Disorder also inhabits the gridded plan and is immediately apparent in the tectonic fractures of the lower Manhattan grids, in the mosaic of grids against the background of the continental grid in Los Angeles, and in the almost imperceptible disturbances of the plan of Chicago. This disorder opens up the possibility of constructing architectural fantasies, that is, the possibility of *inscribing architectural change as permanent traces* that will belong to the long duration of the city. However, the conditions for this *inscription*, that is, for an *architectural articulation* with the city and the particular pleasure produced by it, are found neither in the extreme order of the grid, nor in the complete disorder of its loss, but in the meeting of the borders that separate order and disorder. These sites, where *the articulation of architecture and the city* can take place, are usually found in the space of failure that subverts the permanent traces of the geometric grid and not in the unrestricted spaces where the chaotic and violent urban forces are inscribed.[3]

By constantly reintroducing the question of *the neutral grid*, the urban drawings traverse that fantasy and open up architecture to the failure of the grid, to a wealth of new configurations, of unexpected syntactic constructions and surprising symbolic articulations. Every city demands a specific strategy in the confrontation with architecture. Every city constructs its own questions and its own mode of reception that the urban drawings depict using a multiplicity of techniques of representation. In New York city, the drawings examine the pre-Revolutionary grids in the southern area of Manhattan through the fragmentation of the patchwork of colliding grids and the investigation of their internal logic. In Los Angeles, a similar strategy is employed for the treatment of the city grids, but a delayering depicts the behavior of the one-mile grid in its overlappings and collisions with the local grids and nongridded streets. In Boston, the drawings describe the contrast between two different plan configurations, the European-like fabric versus the overlapping American grids. In New Haven, the drawings depict the plan mostly in terms of the building footprint showing the impact of the original nine-square grid on the surrounding districts and the contrasting formal logic. In Chicago, the drawings explore the behavior of the one-mile grid when it becomes the organizing structure of a city, in particular the local effect of small disturbances. The Des Moines drawings look into the relationships between significant moments, such as public spaces, monumental buildings, or topographic irregularities, and the transitional spaces between the foundation grid and the one-mile grid. Finally, the Atlantic City drawings explore the effects of the X-Urban city of entertainment, a city of casinos, on the deteriorated fabric of the city after the white flight to the neighboring communities, the relationships between dead ends and the fragmentation of the fabric and the relationships of parking in the new coastal strip of casinos and the freeway.

2. Le Corbusier, **When the Cathedrals Were White** (New York: McGraw-Hill, 1964).

3. "Culture and its destruction are not erotic, it is their failure that becomes erotic." Roland Barthes, **The Pleasure of the Text** (New York: Noonday Press, 1980).

## THE URBAN DRAWINGS

The exploration of the plans of New York, Los Angeles, Boston, New Haven, Chicago, Des Moines, and Atlantic City between 1984 and 1994 reveals an ignored formal universe in the American city. Teaching provided an essential space for the production of the urban drawings. In the spring of 1983, I taught a studio at the school of architecture at the University of Illinois where the students were asked to "redraw" the plan of Chicago as an architectural proposition. The project was inspired by a studio that Diana Agrest had taught at the Institute for Architecture and Urban Studies in New York during the mid-1970s, which she based on the notion of "design as reading."[4] The project consisted in developing a formal *parti* found in a given sequence of buildings or urban fragments in Manhattan. The students depicted sequences of buildings or fragments of urban fabric that originally had not been architecturally conceived as such. The process was based on drawings that described only the pertinent elements that belonged to the *parti*, while the features that did not relate to the architectural idea were "edited out."

By working with the plan of Chicago rather than with buildings, my studio, based on the assumption of the autonomy of the plan, "eliminated" the perceptual level and focussed on architectural questions derived from the symptoms, disruptions, and discontinuities that interrupt the continuous spatial flow implied by the grid of streets of the Chicago plan. A process of "visual drifting" allowed us to approach the plan without expectations and without knowing what we were looking for, ensuring that what was found was not what we already knew.[5] The drawings described various situations where dead-ends were produced; for instance, a change in directionality in the service alleys or subtle discontinuities in the grid of streets.

The New York drawings, based on the experience of the Chicago studio of 1983, were developed within the context of the undergraduate studio at the Institute for Architecture and Urban Studies[6] in the fall of the same year. The drawings focused on the gridded sectors that organize the southern area of Manhattan below the 1811 gridiron. The fragmentation of the different grids allowed us to understand overlappings, deformations, and deletions as the multiple effects of the collision of the different grids that represented successive historical developments of the plan. The objectivity of the opposition between figure and ground was subverted by the representation of implied linear continuities, the completion of grid fragments, and the simultaneous representation in two and three dimensions. The opposition between fabric and object-buildings became blurred with the discovery of fabric that acted as object.

Once the New York drawings were completed, I decided to explore the other major American city, Los Angeles, the megalopolis of the West Coast. This study, developed in the context of a seminar at the University of Southern California in Los Angeles, led to the examination of the major role played by the one-mile grid as the "glue" linking all the different cities and towns included in Los Angeles, and the

4. Agrest, "Design vs. Non-designed," in Agrest, *Architecture from Without.*

5. See the discussion of reading mechanism in chapter 3.

6. The program operated with the collaboration of David Moohney. The studio faculty included Deborah Gans, Paul Gates, Michael Stanton, Pat Sapinsley, and myself, as the director. The raw material produced by the studio was redrawn during the summer of 1984 by Michael Stanton, with the collaboration of Nancy Clayton and Allan Organsky.

specific typological behavior of the American city where the building type acts as the imaginary origin of a transformational structure as opposed to a frozen structural configuration that characterizes the European urban building typology.[7]

The next three sets of drawings looked into Boston, New Haven, and Chicago. While Boston started with an irregular radio-concentric plan that developed into a gridded condition during the nineteenth century, New Haven's regular foundation plan, a nine-square grid, developed into an irregular radio-concentric plan.[8] A second studio in Chicago provided the opportunity to inspect an apparently exclusively single-grid plan. This condition changed the method: instead of looking for regularities in irregular plans, I looked for irregularities concealed by the grid. Chicago also marks the point where, in 1989, I started to work with the computer in the context of the Chicago Institute for Architecture and Urbanism under the direction of John Whiteman.[9] The use of the computer opened new theoretical questions and facilitated the production of "cinematic" sequences, where certain features were deleted, added, or altered.

The analytical drawings of Des Moines developed in a different context with respect to the previous cities. They were part of a project that attempted to examine the possibility of articulating the drawings with a practice of *rewriting* the American city, what became the Des Moines Vision Plan. As part of the process, the urban drawings had a crucial role in the communication with the community but also acted as an armature against which some of the designs were developed. Finally, the drawings of Atlantic City looked into a paradigmatic X-Urban condition, a city transformed by the entertainment industry into a gambling touristic center. The drawings attempt to represent the traumatic implications of this change for urban form.

7. The Los Angeles drawings were redrawn during the summer of 1985 by Kris Kapeller who was one of the students in the seminar where the original drawings were produced.

8. The Boston drawings were realized in the context of a seminar taught at Harvard University on two different occasions. The New Haven drawings were realized in the context of a design studio at the school of architecture at Yale University, with the collaboration of Kevin Kennon as a teaching assistant.

9. The drawings were produced with the assistance of Julie Wheeler and published in Mario Gandelsonas, *The Urban Text* (Cambridge, Mass.: The MIT Press, 1992).

# Cities

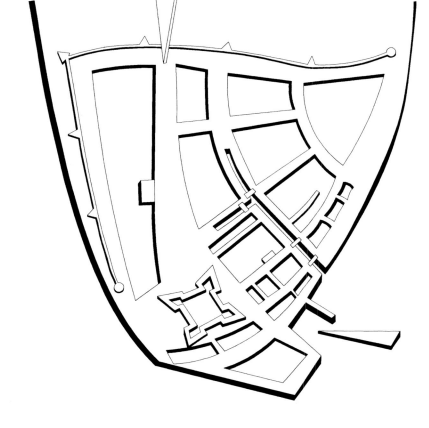

*The drawings examine six different representations of
New York that precede the 1811 gridiron, showing the
development of the plan below the gridiron.*

## THE RADIO-CONCENTRIC CITY BELOW THE GRIDIRON
### PLAN 1

The plan is organized by a north-south street that separates two morphological structures: a radial structure of blocks with its center on the northeast, and a long block organized by an orthogonal structure revealed by
the property lines and an open square on the west. The east side of the
street opens up, determined by the radial structure, transforming the
street into a field occupied by the fort.

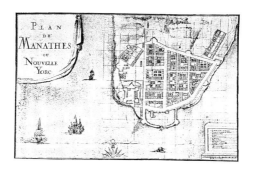

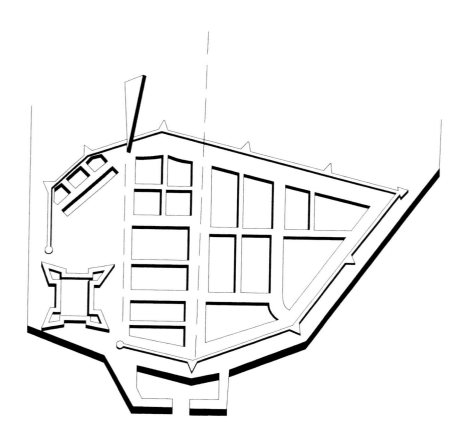

## PLAN 2

This plan proposes an alternative fictional reading of New Amsterdam.
In this case, the plan is still conceived in terms of two structures, proving
that the dichotomy read in the first map is a strong structural feature.
The radial zone is now seen as a grid. The western sector is seen as a
field with objects: the fort, a skewed urban block, and buildings.

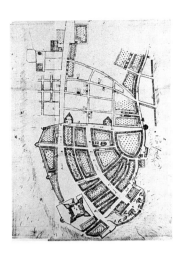

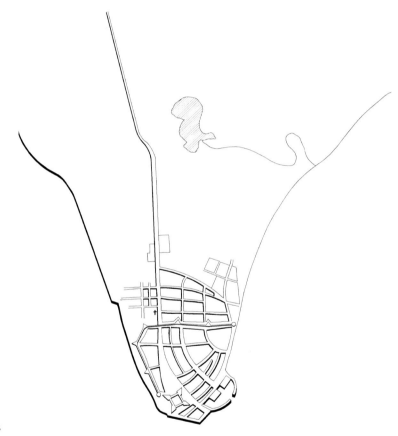

**PLAN 3**

The plan presents the first potential extension beyond the city walls
where a double concentric system is implied. This is an ambiguous
stage where the dominance of either radial system is not clear.
The western edge within the wall is absorbed into the radial system.
However, Broadway generates again an orthogonal system on the
west side above the wall.

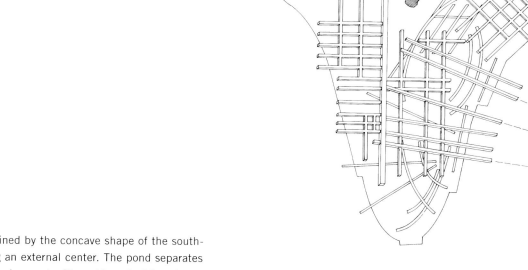

## PLAN 4

A new radial system is defined by the concave shape of the south-
eastern coastline, implying an external center. The pond separates
the east- and west-side developments. The grid west of Broadway
is more established and seems to extend into the east side.

## PLAN 5

New grids develop following the coastline in both the Hudson and
the East Rivers. An oblique grid extending west of Lafayette Street is
established. Broadway becomes an axis for the development of a
north-south grid that prefigures the orientation of the 1811 gridiron,
although not its strong east-west directionality.

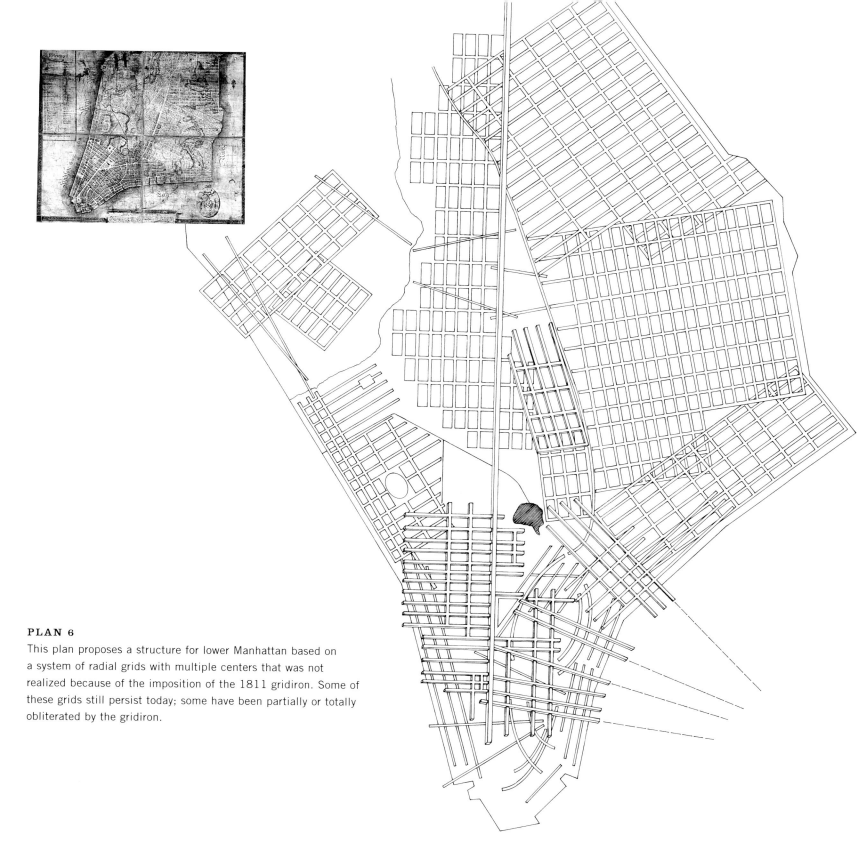

**PLAN 6**

This plan proposes a structure for lower Manhattan based on
a system of radial grids with multiple centers that was not
realized because of the imposition of the 1811 gridiron. Some of
these grids still persist today; some have been partially or totally
obliterated by the gridiron.

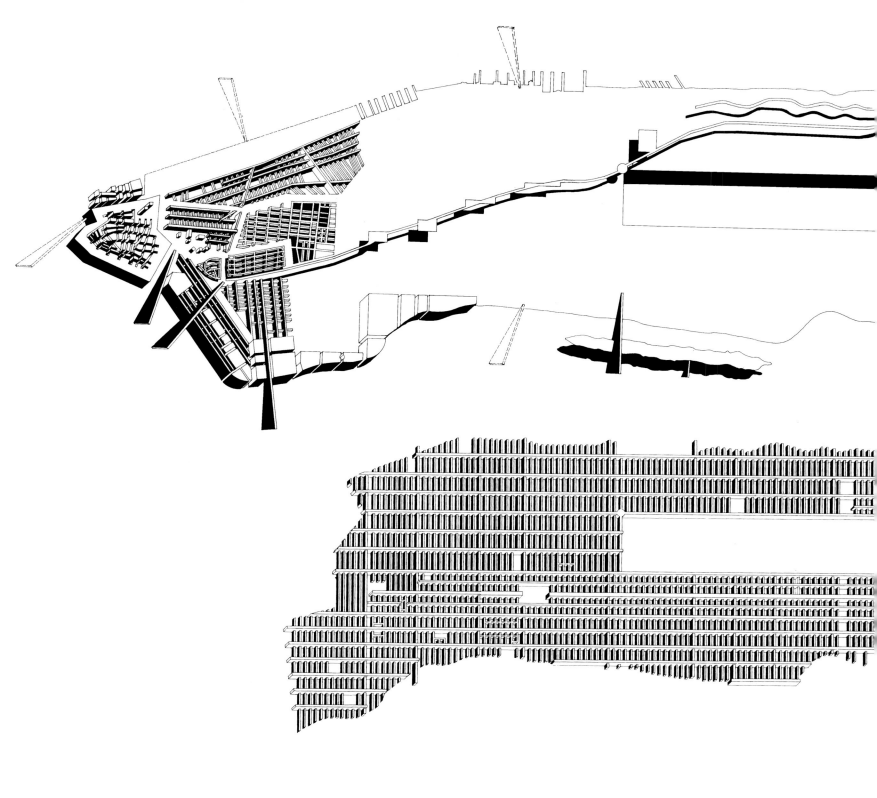

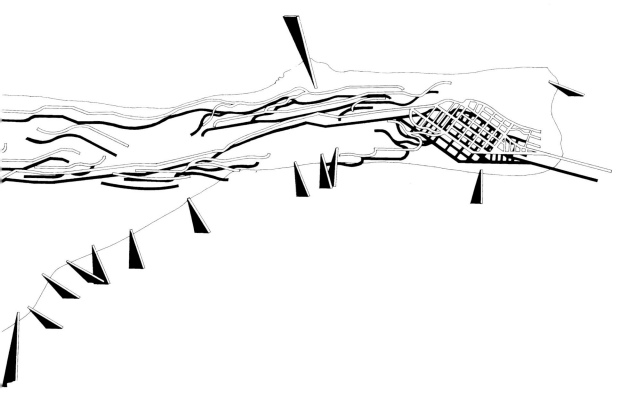

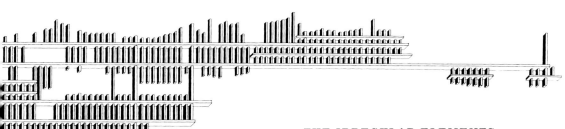

## THE IRREGULAR ELEMENTS
### PLAN 7:
### THE PLAN MINUS THE GRIDIRON

The subtraction of the post-Revolutionary grid-iron reveals the major significant urban situations articulating the formal structure of Manhattan. The dominant features are the open space of Central Park versus the urban fabric (the absent gridiron); the collisions of the pre-Revolutionary grids in the southern tip of the island; the topographically determined system of north-south streets in the northwestern area that culminate in the diamond grid of the northern tip; and Broadway, which acts as a link between these diverse situations. The intersection of Broadway and the wide east-west streets produce a necklace of public spaces: Union Square at 14th Street, Herald Square at 34th Street, Times Square at 42nd Street, and Columbus Circle at 59th Street. Bridges and tunnels connect the island and puncture its fabric in a random way.

### PLAN 8: THE GRIDIRON

Long, narrow blocks characterize most of the gridiron, with two major exceptions: first, a strip east of Fifth Avenue to Third Avenue where Madison and Lexington Avenues divide the long blocks into square blocks and, second, upper Manhattan where the topographic irregularities translated into the street system fragment the gridiron.

## THE PLAN BELOW THE GRIDIRON
## PLAN 9: THE POCHE PLAN

The "poche" plan (where city blocks and building-objects have been represented as solids) describes the difference between the compact fabric and the fields of "building-objects" in the plan of Manhattan: the super-block of the World Trade Center, the monumental *forum* that includes Foley and Federal Squares, the housings of the East River edge, and the New York University housing on La Guardia Place.

## PLAN 10:
## FRAGMENTATION OF THE PLAN

How do we start the analysis of the irregular plan? By fracturing the "text," by breaking up the area into smaller sectors with recognizable patterns. This operation makes visible the distortions and transformations of the different grids.

The plan of lower Manhattan now includes the "perfect grid" versus the irregularities, areas reflecting major grid tendencies, and

intermediate or transitional areas. Of the four areas defining the edge, sectors 1, 7, and 8 present grids that relate to the docks and sector 4 relates to the Williamsburg Bridge that penetrates the area. The central area was subsequently divided into four sectors, two on the west, two on the east. The two western areas present orthogonal grids with different directionalities: sector 2 is north-south and sector 5 is east-west. The two eastern areas contain intermediate fabrics that reflect different mediating formal operations such as convergence compression and bending. The sectors are drawn in two and three dimensions representing overlapping streets and grids, intersections, and hierarchical distinctions, between streets and avenues.

## PLAN 11: SECTOR 1A

The northern area of this sector is defined by three grids "fanning out" in a radio-concentric manner and cutting into the gridiron. North-south avenues parallel to the Hudson River are

woven throughout the fan. The rest of the sector is defined by a system of streets determined by the direction of the docks. Canal Street slices through the sector, indifferent to its structure.

## PLAN 12: SECTOR 1B

The sectional hierarchy incorporated in the solid/void (high/low) reversal of streets clarifies relationships and adds a new level of information.

## PLAN 13: SECTOR 2A

The northern area of this sector seems to result from the overlapping of the gridiron and the SoHo grid. The superimposition of the two grids "produces" the square blocks adjacent to Washington Square Park that act as a formal transition between the grids.

## PLAN 14: SECTOR 2B

The north-south streets (Avenue of the Americas, La Guardia Place, Broadway, and Lafayette) and east-west streets (Houston and Canal Streets) act as edges of superblocks

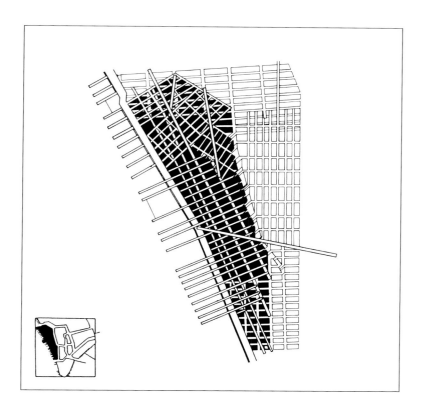

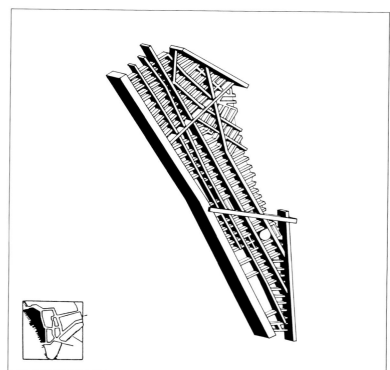

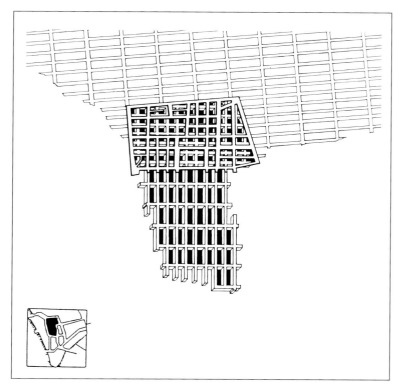

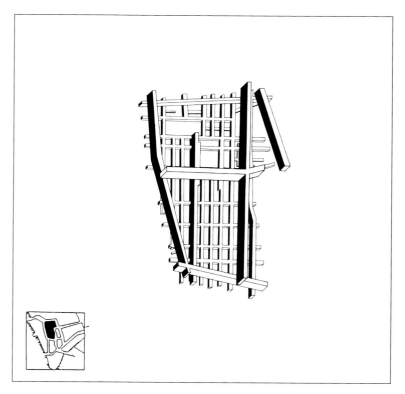

**PLAN 15: SECTOR 3A**
This sector is structured on the basis of a grid
compressed in the east-west axis between SoHo
and the East Village. The Williamsburg and
Manhattan Bridges and Canal Street suggest a
field of forces that explains the positioning of
the different grids and their specific action on
this sector.

**PLAN 16: SECTOR 3B**
The compression of this sector is described as
the effect of the overlapping of sectors 2 and 4.

**PLAN 18: SECTOR 4A**
This drawing presents a fictional version of a
permeable grid for Williamsburg, Brooklyn,
which in reality is totally opaque to the irongrid.
There is a major reason for this opacity: the
intrusion of the Williamsburg Bridge as a
skewer through the grid.

**PLAN 19: SECTOR 4B**
In this sector the fabric is interrupted by a field
with object-buildings (housing projects) before
it reaches the East River. The buildings are
represented as voids carved from a five-story
solid representing the razed fabric.

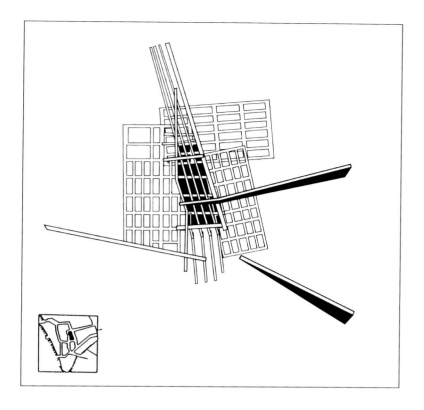

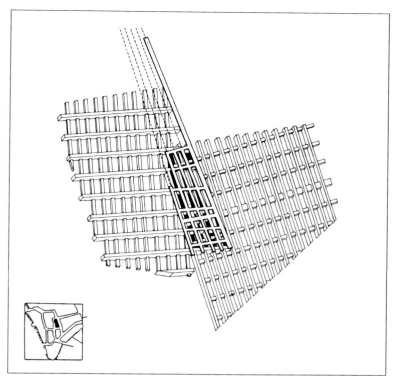

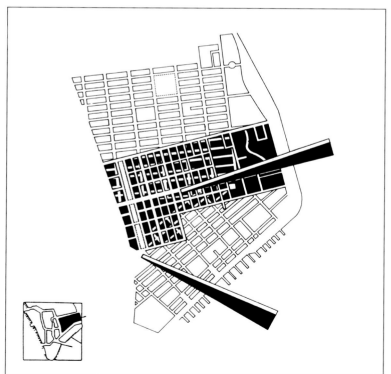

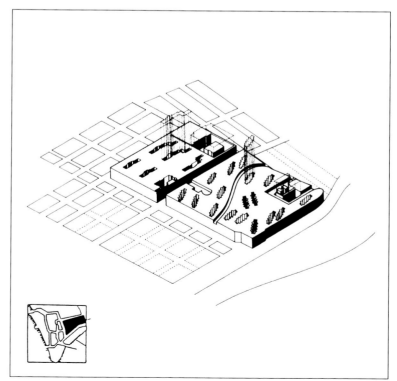

**PLAN 20: SECTOR 5A**

The penetration of the Brooklyn Bridge into
Manhattan produces an explosive situation
where the fabric is mutated into a field with
objects. Broadway (again) is the line of resistance that stops that force. However, three
streets and the fabric that generates them man-
age to cross the Broadway barrier into the vast
triangular forum pushing against the edges the
drifting monumental buildings.

**PLAN 21: SECTOR 5B**

Canal Street and the Manhattan Bridge are the
thresholds between the northern urban fabric
and the southern field with building-objects.

**PLAN 22: SECTOR 6A**

This is another transitional sector where the
grid bends. Distorted by the pressure of neighboring sectors, the grid ignores Canal Street but
is affected by the East River grid and pressured
by the impact of the Manhattan Bridge.

**PLAN 23: SECTOR 6B**

Broadway acts as the threshold between the
western urban fabric and the eastern field with
building-objects.

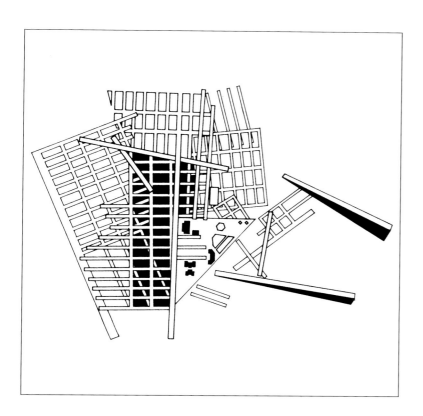

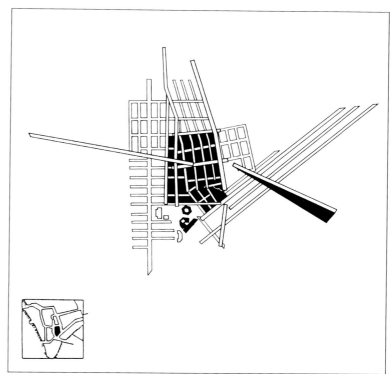

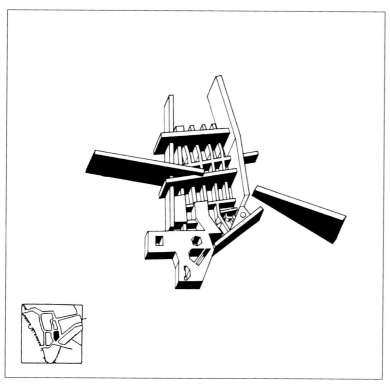

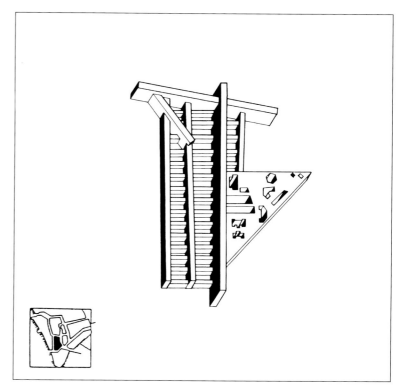

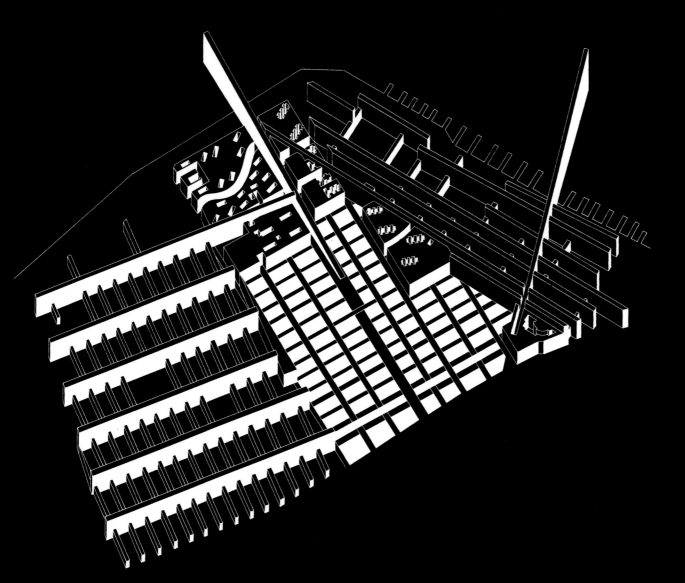

**PLAN 24: SECTOR 7A**
The Manhattan Bridge is indifferent to the direction of the grid, and cuts across this sector.

**PLAN 25: SECTOR 7B**
The urban fabric in this sector has been replaced with objects "floating" in a field.

**PLAN 26: SECTOR 8**
The square field created by the World Trade Center complements the circular field of Battery Park and the triangular field of Foley Square.

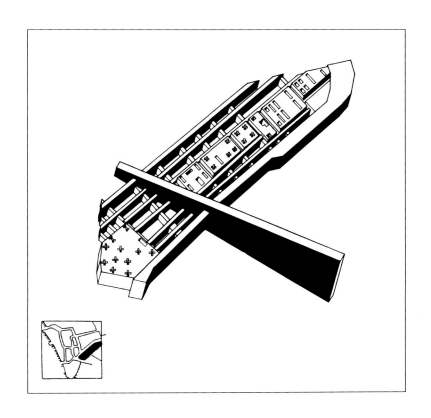

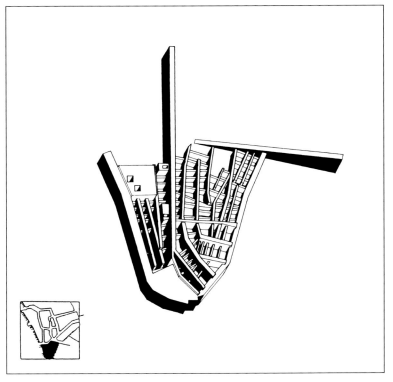

Los Angeles

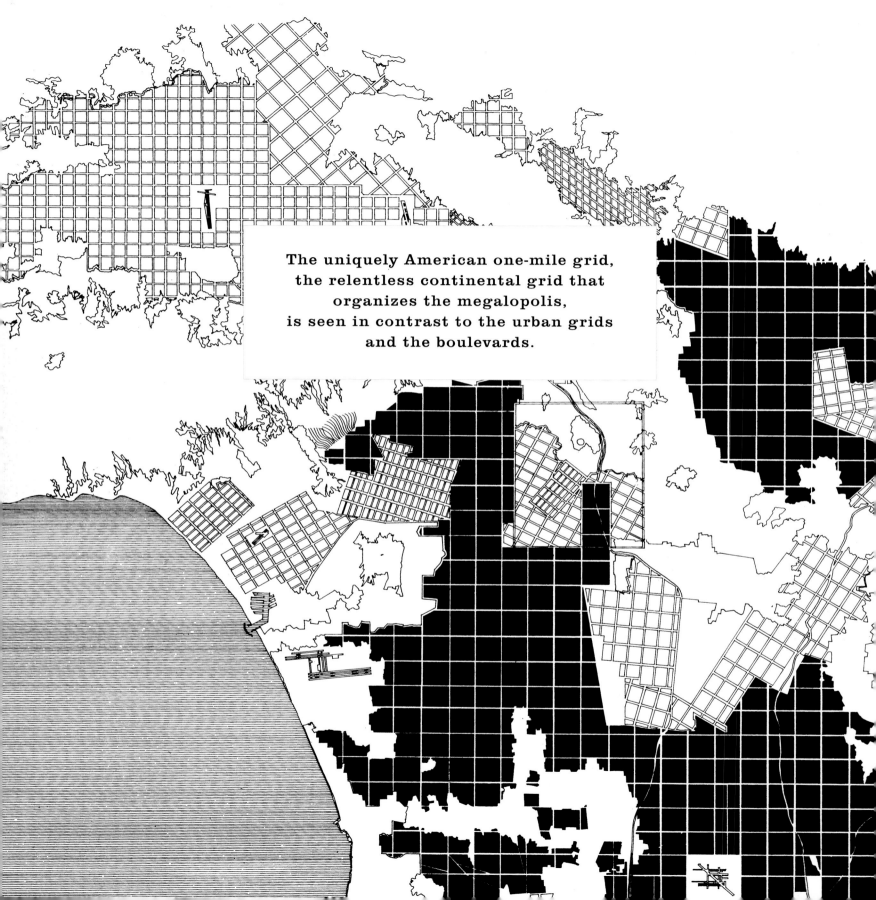

The uniquely American one-mile grid,
the relentless continental grid that
organizes the megalopolis,
is seen in contrast to the urban grids
and the boulevards.

## PLAN 1:
## THE TERRITORIAL GRID

The perceived chaos of the Los Angeles plan obscures a complex system combining city grids as colossal city fabrics as objects (laid out at different angles) with the one-mile grid as background (acting as a "glue" between the different cities). The one-mile grid is interrupted by the hills appearing as topographic accidents of the horizontal plane: the gridded morphology, the historical pueblo grid, the city grids, the one-mile grid, and the hills (the nongridded morphology).

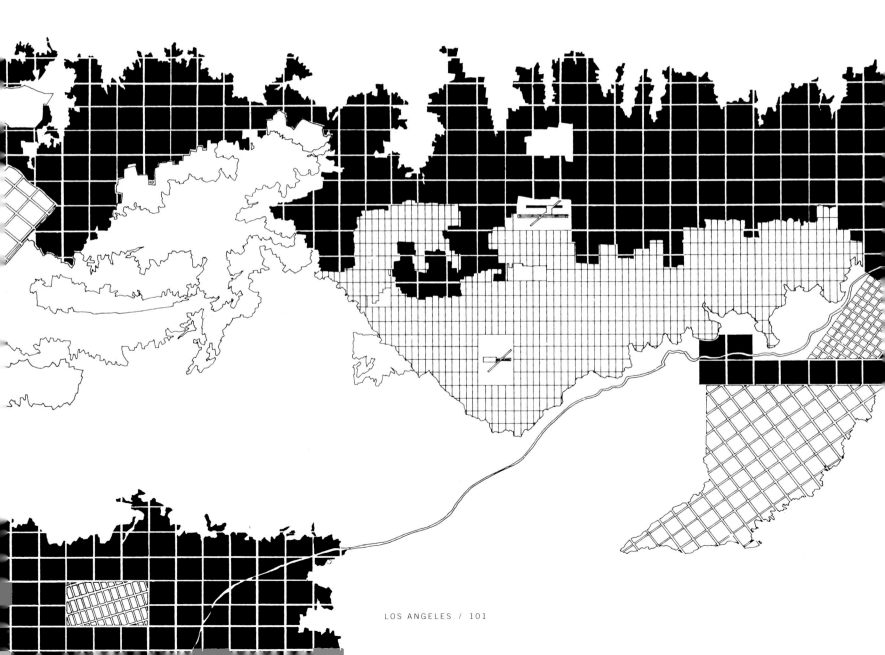

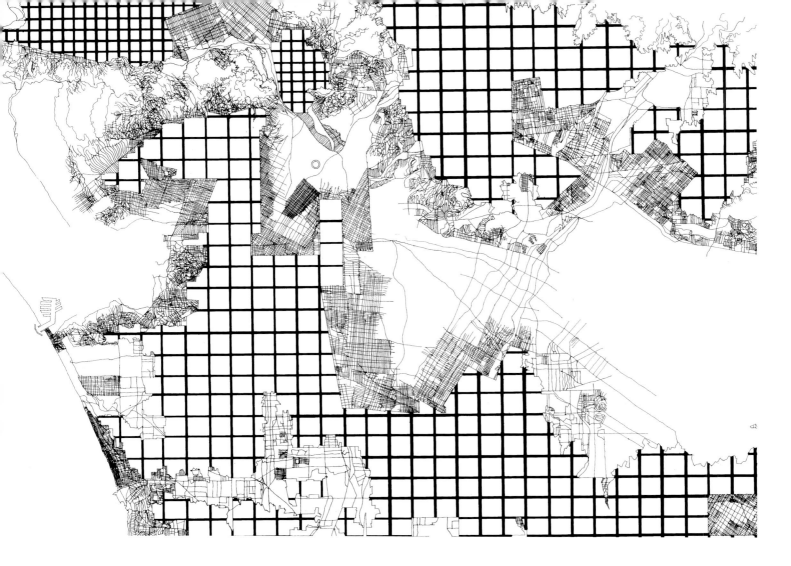

**PLAN 2:**
**SANTA MONICA, BEVERLY HILLS,**
**AND LOS ANGELES**
A close-up view reestablishes the Los Angeles collage clarified by the previous drawing. The colossal scale of the one-mile grid, the hills, and the ocean as datum makes the Los Angeles plan understandable.

**PLAN 3:**
**THE LOS ANGELES MEGACITY**
This drawing presents the opposition between the one-mile grid and a complex morphology that condensates the historical (the gridded cities) and the geographical (the hills).

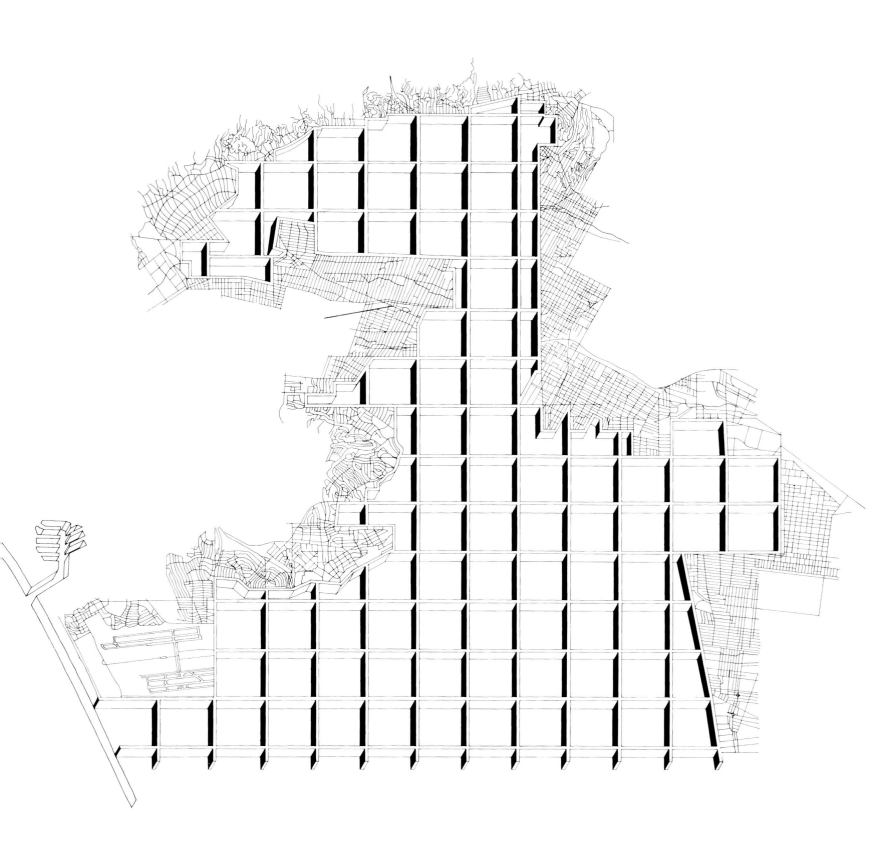

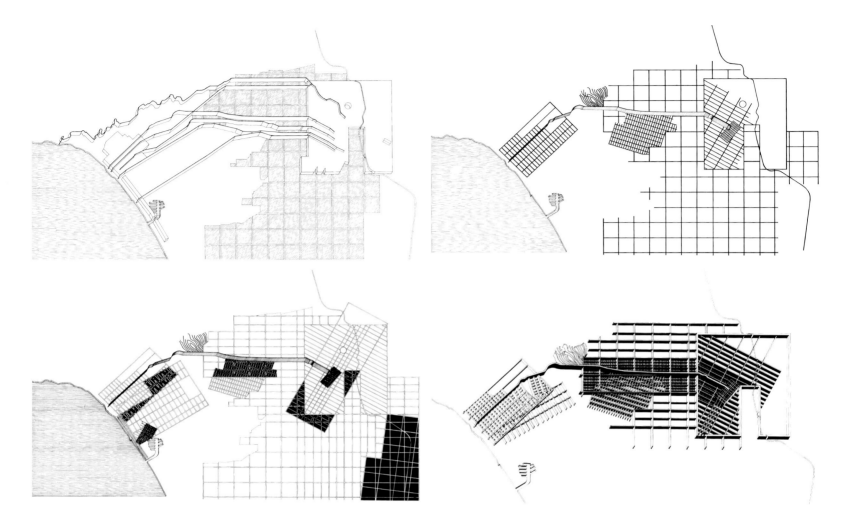

**PLAN 4:**
**THE BOULEVARDS**
The boulevards are the flows of energy that act as connectors between the different elements of the Los Angeles plan. They are shown as linear walls as if the flows had been channeled through the grids, both the explicit and the absent city grids.

**PLAN 5:**
**GRID RELATIONSHIPS: WILSHIRE BOULEVARD AND THE CITY GRIDS**
This is the first of a series of drawings representing Wilshire Boulevard. Different modes of relationship between the boulevard and the city grids are made explicit: bisecting or framing, acknowledging or ignoring, going across or stopping.

**PLAN 6:**
**TWO-DIMENSIONAL GRID INTERSECTIONS**
In the second Wilshire Boulevard drawing the grids engage in a play with adjacent grids. The overlappings should be seen as fictions that might have a certain explanatory role (i.e., the "reason" for certain irregularities in the behavior of the city grids and/or the boulevard's trajectory).

**PLAN 7:**
**THREE-DIMENSIONAL GRID INTERSECTIONS**
In the third Wilshire Boulevard drawing, the three-dimensional representation is presented.

**PLAN 8: GRID PUZZLE**
The fourth drawing represents Wilshire Boulevard with the different city grids as a puzzle "hovering" above the "real" plan of Los Angeles. The boulevard bisects or presents an edge for the different city plan(e)s.

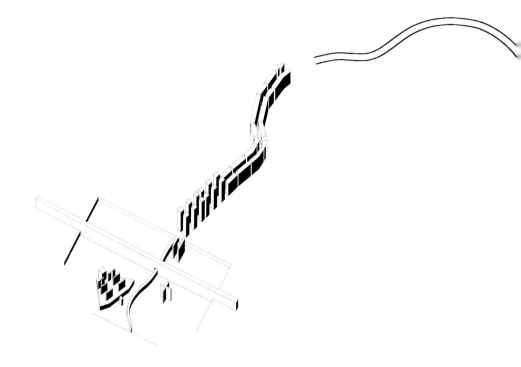

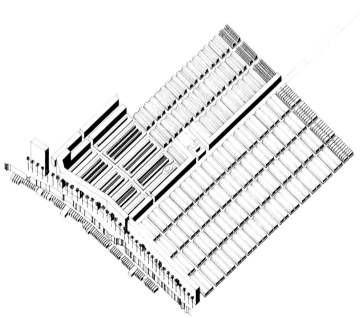

## PLAN 9: TYPOLOGICAL TRANSFORMATION

This is the first of a series of typological descriptions of the different urban landscapes along Wilshire Boulevard, one of the first high-rise corridors, a canyon as opposed to the traditional high-rise hill associated with Manhattan. Santa Monica is literally bisected by Wilshire Boulevard.

## PLAN 10: CROSSING THE 405

The drawing represents two conditions. In the first, the freeway, a linear object, cuts across a field of objects bisected by Whilshire Boulevard represented as solid; in the second, Wilshire is defined by the walls of the high-rise corridor that start at that point.

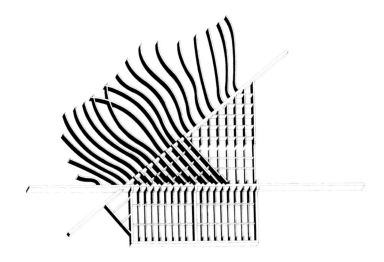

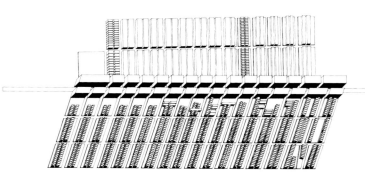

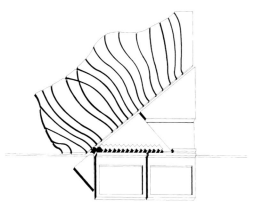

## PLAN 11: BEVERLY HILLS (1)

Beverly Hills is one of the most extraordinary morphological structures in Los Angeles. The undulating streets provide a unique and distinctive treatment of the transition between the flat grid and the hills.

## PLAN 12: BEVERLY HILLS (2)

From a typological point of view, Beverly Hills provides a second example of Wilshire not as a room but as an edge, not as a space but as boundary between districts, where every side of the street is different.

## PLAN 13: THE HIGH-RISE WALL

The drawing shows "degree zero function" of the Wilshire Boulevard high-rise wall, the "walling" of adjacent low-rise districts characterized by a fabric made up of single-family houses.

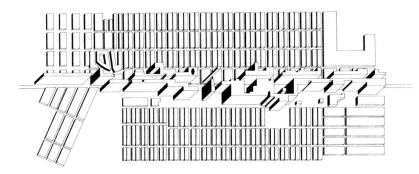

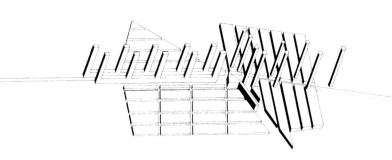

**PLAN 14:**
**MORPHOLOGICAL/TYPOLOGICAL**
**RELATIONSHIPS**

A diptych of opposing directional grids and high-rise building types can be implied from the existing street pattern and buildings. Base-attached towers sit on the east-west biased grid while the floating towers sit on the north-south grid.

**PLAN 15:**
**DEVELOPMENT**

A new fabric develops as a result of the formation of the high-rise canyon. The need for parking erodes the first block behind the wall. The wall itself becomes more objectlike — a thick wall with a more formal front and sculptural recesses in the back — that is no longer embedded in the contiguous fabric.

**PLAN 16: EISENHOWER PARK**

This park is the point of departure of a sequence of building objects, urban spaces and low-rise fabric that act as a "pause" between the high-rise canyon (Wilshire Boulevard) and the high-rise hill (downtown Los Angeles)

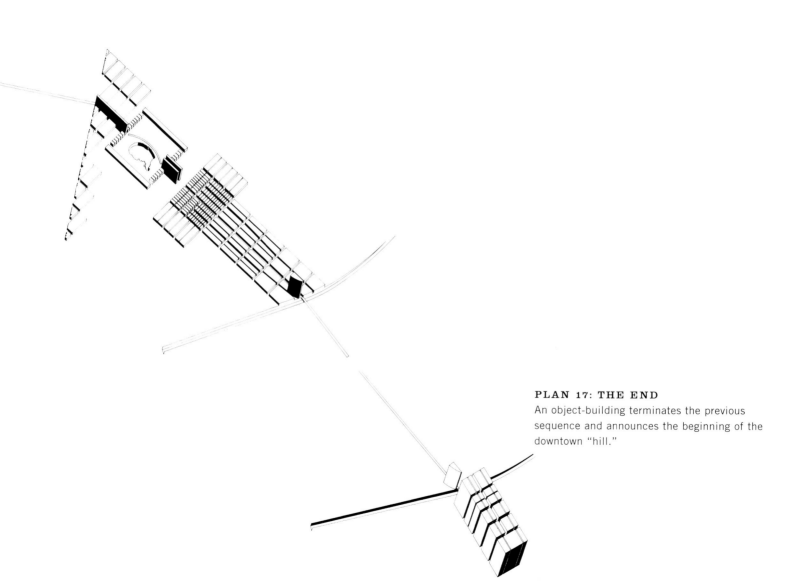

**PLAN 17: THE END**
An object-building terminates the previous
sequence and announces the beginning of the
downtown "hill."

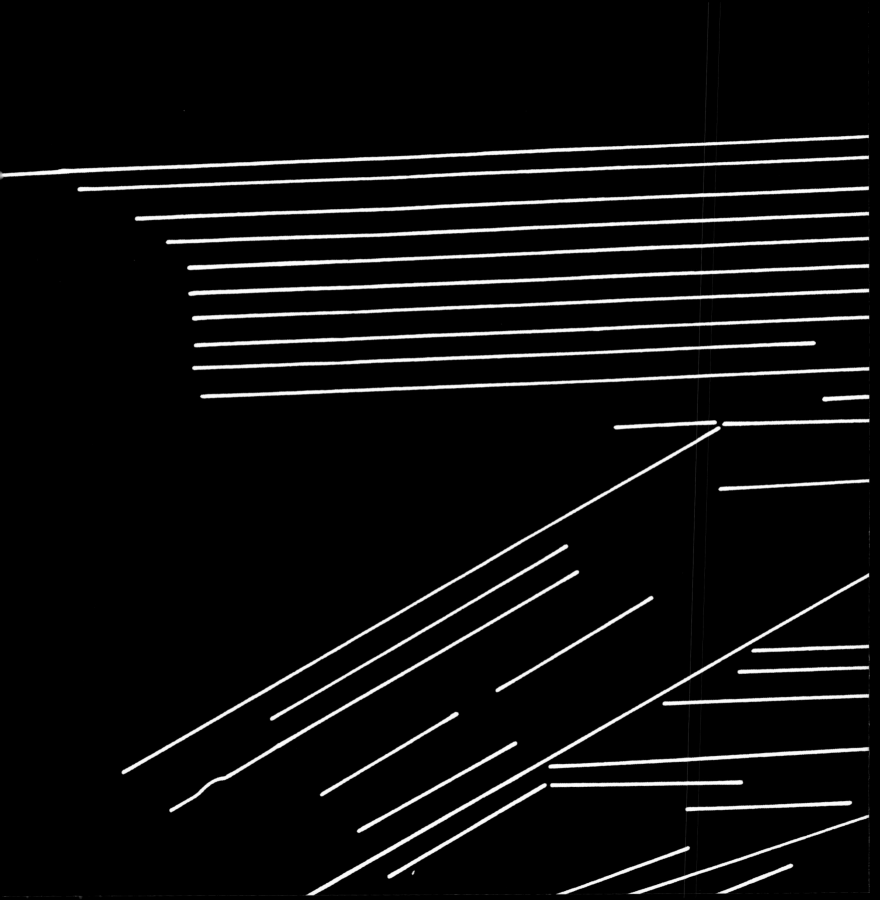

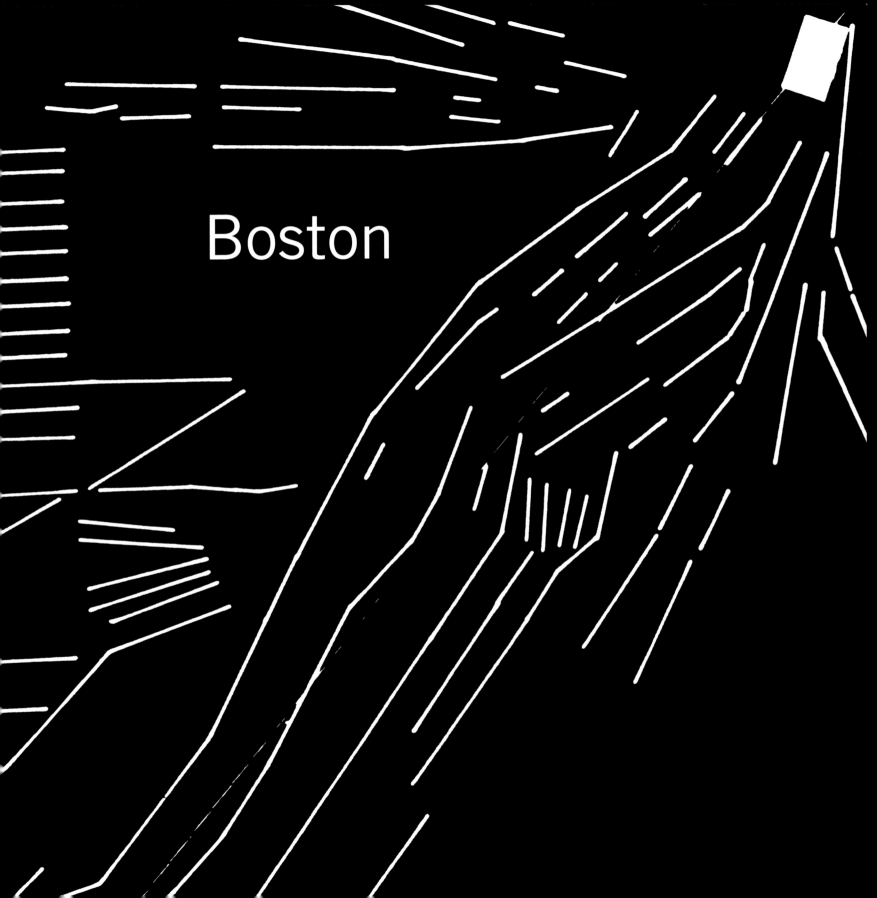

## THE HEAD AND THE NECK

Alternating sectors of urban fabric and fields
— with or without building objects —
form the "head" of Boston.
The "neck" can be seen as the result of
the overlapping of different grids.
Interventions made after World War II have deeply
affected the morphology of Boston,
erasing entire areas of the close-knit fabric
of the seventeenth and eighteenth centuries and
replacing them with modernist-inspired
building developments.
The result is a series of discontinuous radial sectors
of fabric alternating with sectors of objects in a field
revealed by the analytical drawings.
The peculiar topographic history of Boston
(the leveling of hills and the filling of Back Bay)
might partially explain the different degrees
of resistance to change that characterize
the historical fabric of Beacon Hill, for instance.

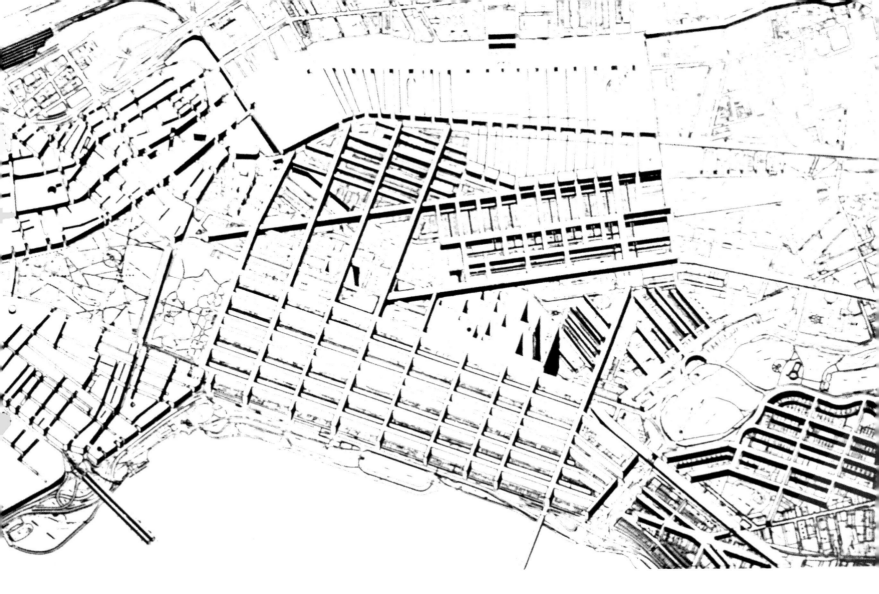

**PLAN 1: THE PLAN OF BOSTON**
The major structural elements of the city, fabric, fields with object-buildings, and grids are described as an artificially uniform extrusion overlapped onto the plan of Boston as a background.

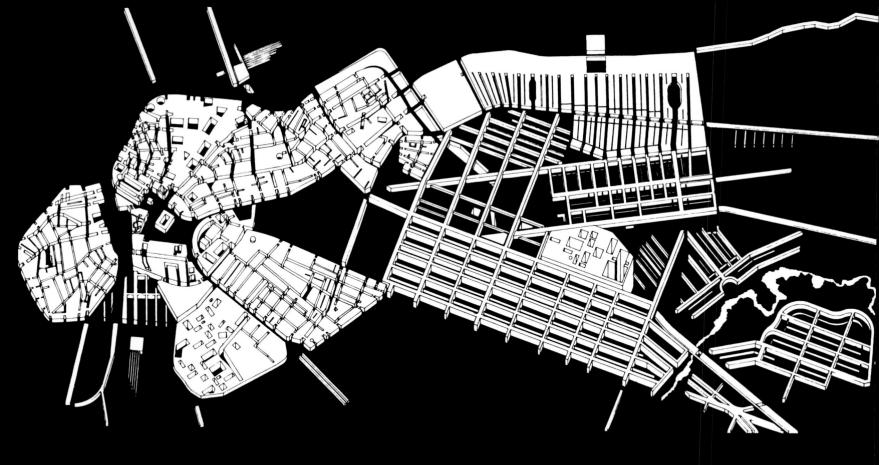

**PLAN 2:**
**THE STRUCTURAL ELEMENTS**
In a process of delayering, the plan of actual
streets is dropped and only the structural
elements are described.

**PLAN 3a-b:**
**TRIANGULAR LEFTOVERS**
The radio-concentric structure is disturbed by the
orthogonal grids of the individual sectors and by
the topographic and programmatic boundaries of
the various precincts. These areas of disturbance
can be represented as a series of triangular residual spaces — as an urbanization of nonstructural,
interstitial areas or punctuations.

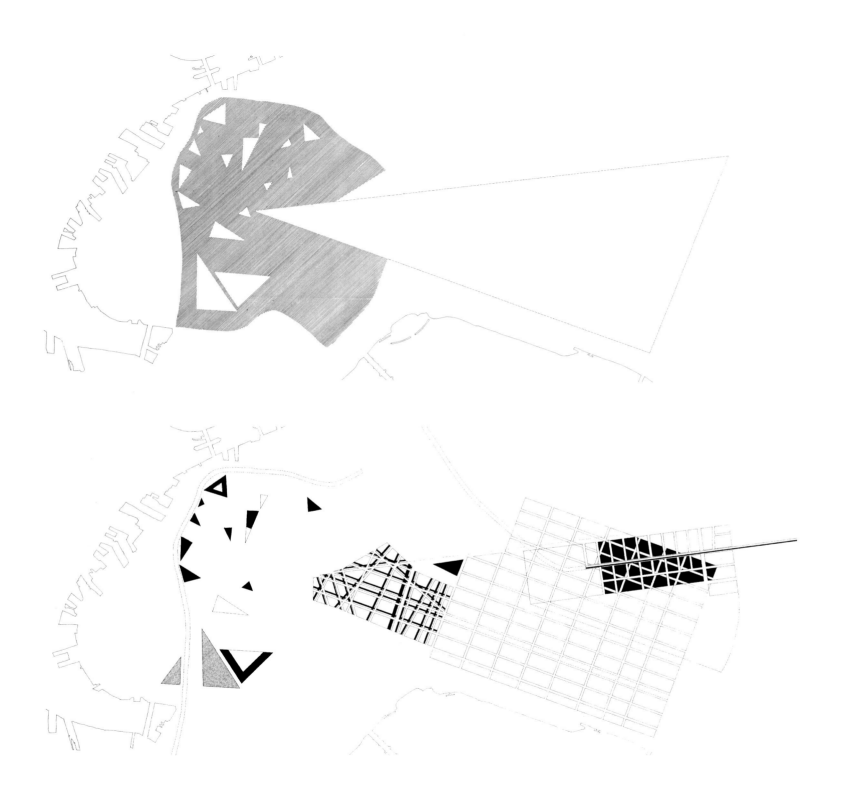

**PLAN 4:**

**THE RADIO-CONCENTRIC STRUCTURE**

The poche plan presents a chaotic assemblage of regular and distorted (geometric and organic) grids. The delayering of the poche plan clearly depicts the radial versus the circumferential streets.

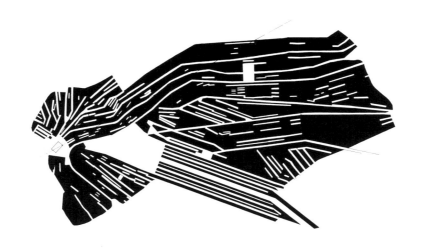

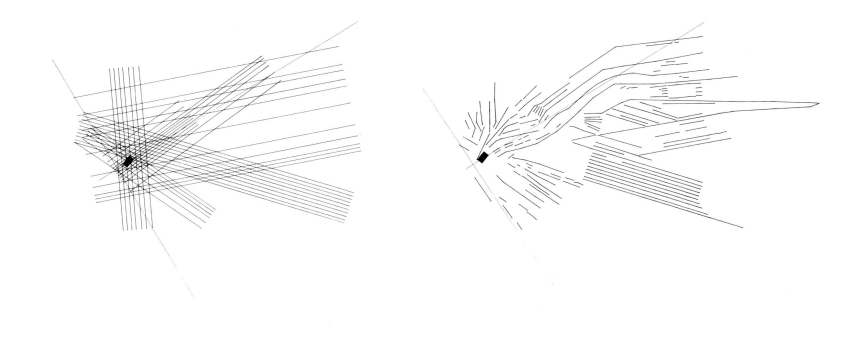

## PLAN 5:
### THE RADIAL SYSTEM

The original radio-concentric structure is the organizing force of Boston's major urban elements, fabric, objects and expressway. The radial street system — more that the corresponding circumferential street system — is the expression of that force. This hierarchy is present both in the "head" and in the "neck" of Boston and gives order both to the fabric and to the object buildings. This is true even in the Back Bay, which operates structurally as a radial sector and not as a discrete area.

**a.** Patterns of radial streets, circumferential streets, and the resultant block pattern with Boston's City Hall as an implied center

**b.** Streets in the head and the neck that belong to the radial system

**c.** Streets in the neck that belong to the radial system

**d.** Figure-ground reversal of fabric and object buildings in the Back Bay, the Prudential Center, and the South End

**e.** The Back Bay, the Prudential Center, and the South End as sectors of the radial system

**f.** Systematic relationships of fabric and object-buildings depicted by the axis of buildings

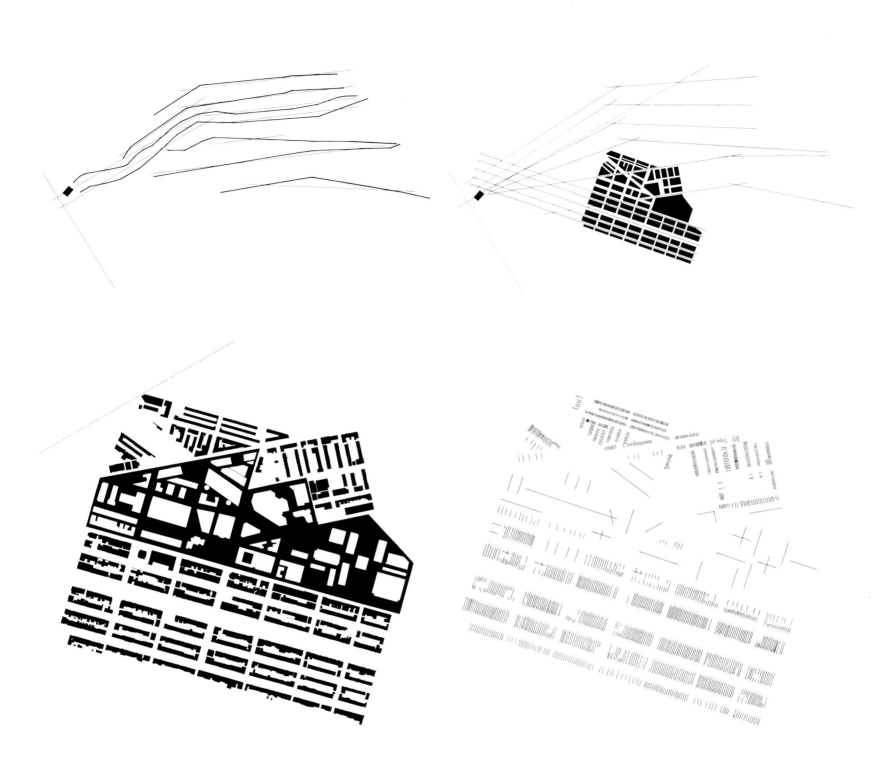

New Haven

The original plan of New Haven contained
elements that should both insure the survival of
the original grid — an oversized nine-square grid
(825 total square feet) with a common green
in the center — while also generating a new order
for its development, several diagonal streets
leading outward from the core.
This radial field system surrounding the nine-square
grid persists in the plan of New Haven today.
However, this description represents only a simple,
perceptual understanding of the city.

PLAN 1:
FABRIC AND OBJECTS
The erasure of the fabric and its replacement with building objects have created in New Haven a situation similar to Boston: an alternation of sector of fabric and fields with objects. The original-nine-square grid as the conceptual center of the city that has now lost its formal balance is still the element that establishes the identity of New Haven.

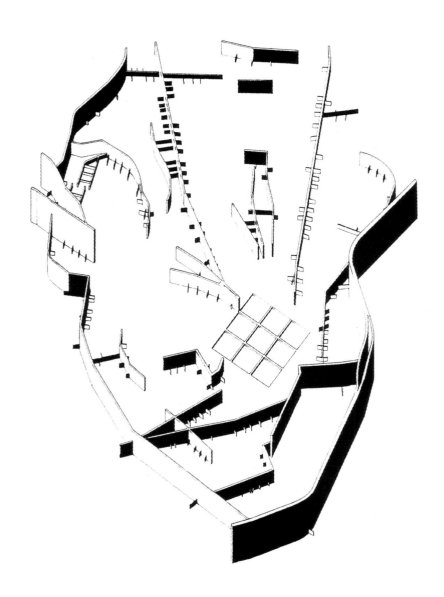

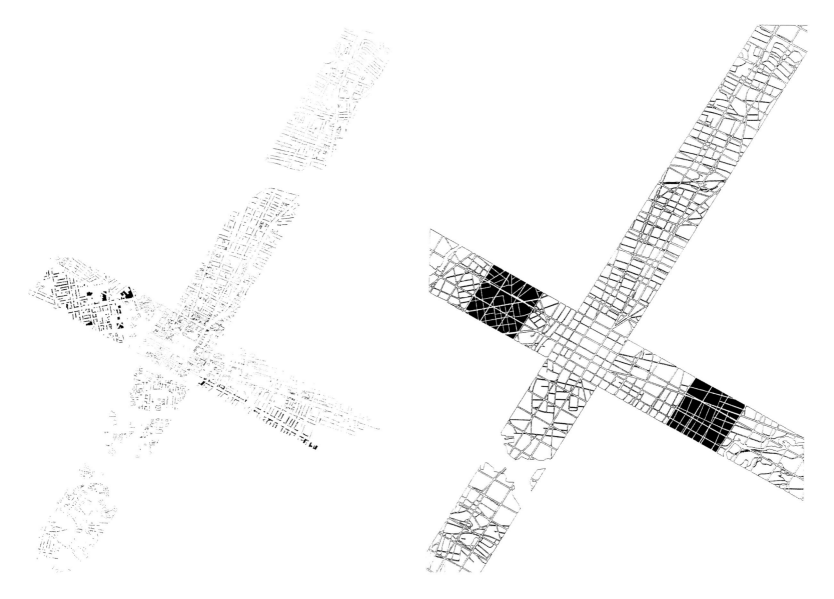

**PLAN 2:**
**INVISIBLE WALLS**
The radio-concentric development of New Haven around the original nine-square grid produces a structure of layered implied walls as fault lines where the radial streets break or dead end. The invisible walls reinforce the reading of the nine-square grid and not just the green as a center.

**PLANS 3 AND 4:**
**THE CROSS**
The arbitrary extension of the nine-square grid to form a cross that cuts through the plan reveals in a different way the radio-concentric movement around the static center first with the streets and then with the buildings.

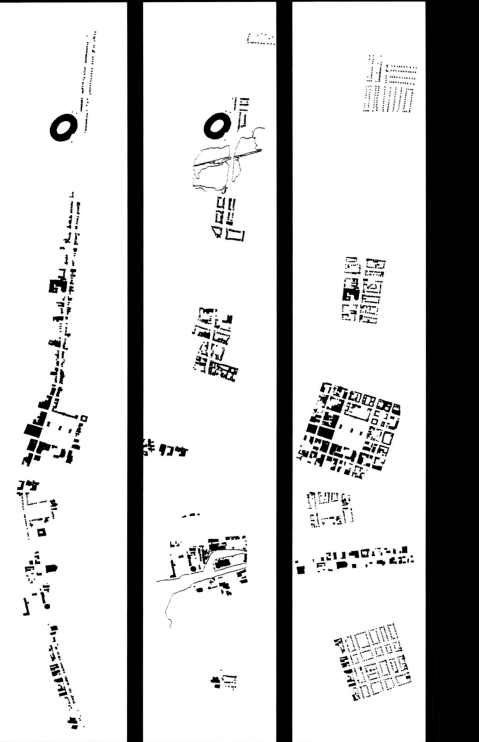

## PLANS 5, 6, AND 7:
## STRING OF VILLAGES

At the level of buildings, order is not just
confined to the campus. A number of different
typological structures are organized according to
a rigorous urban logic. The drawings depict the
role of Chapel Street as a mechanism that
strings together gridded areas of fabric of different densities alternating with a series of irregular
fabrics or building objects such as the stadium.
The first drawing represents the typological
sequence along Chapel Street, the second the
regular grids and the third the irregular elements
producing an abacada sequence.

## PLAN 8: DISSOLVING DENSITIES

The opposition of central grid versus circumferential fabric is redoubled by the opposition
between the attached buildings forming continuous and impermeable street walls versus the
scattered object buildings forming discontinuous
and porous street walls.

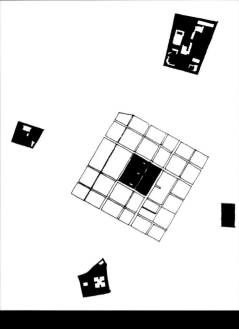

## PLAN 9: CLONING
The drawing describes a variety of effects produced by the tension between the different formal order of the square core and the radio-concentric organization of the surrounding fabric. They propose that the identity of New Haven is defined by the set of urban formal structures and processes of which the strongest feature is a "family" of grids cloned from their core and rotating as satellites around it. Traces of four potential squares can be found in the radio-concentric area surrounding the central grid and replicating the green.

## PLAN 10:
### THE FICTIONAL ONE-MILE GRID
There was never a one-mile grid in New Hav However its displacement and overlapping v the city allows us to read a multiplicity of u conditions concealed by the organizing pow of the radio-concentric configuration.

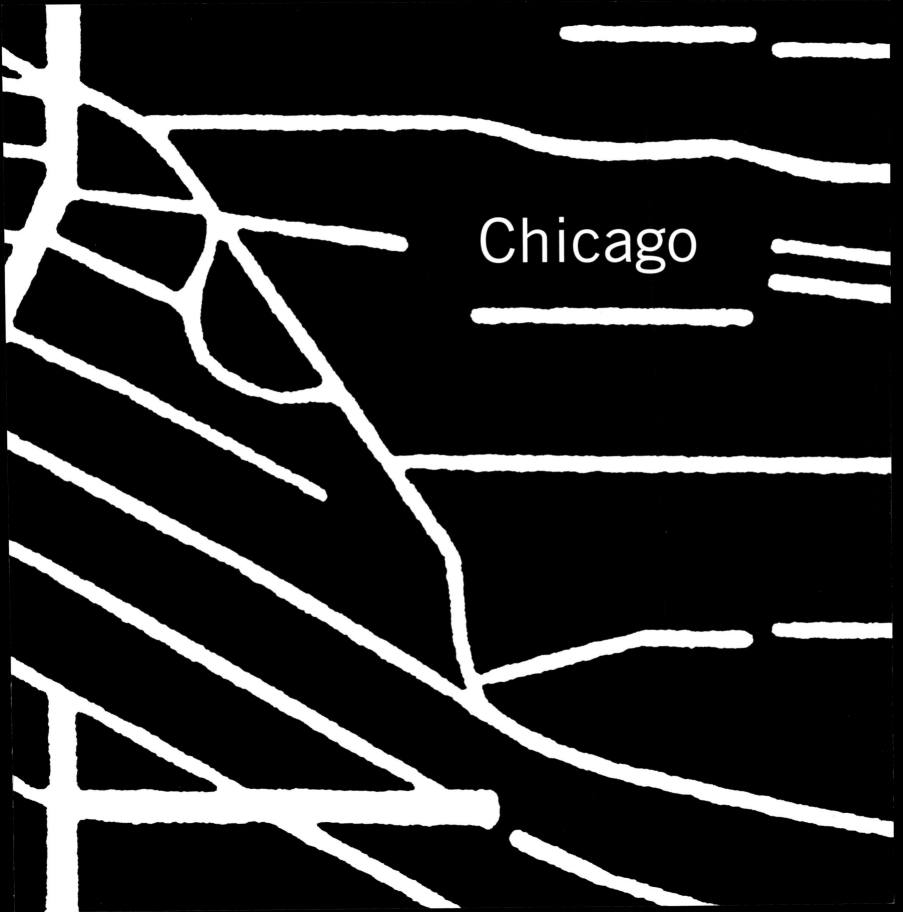

While the neutral geometric grid
and the regular "beat" of intersections in the city of
Chicago imply continuous movement,
the "accidents" of the plan produce
changing rhythms and interruptions
where movement stops.

## THE INK DRAWINGS

The series of ink drawings examine two
situations that produce these
interruptions of the one-mile grid:
the effect of the multiple diagonals
that crisscross the plan,
and the effect of topographic changes.

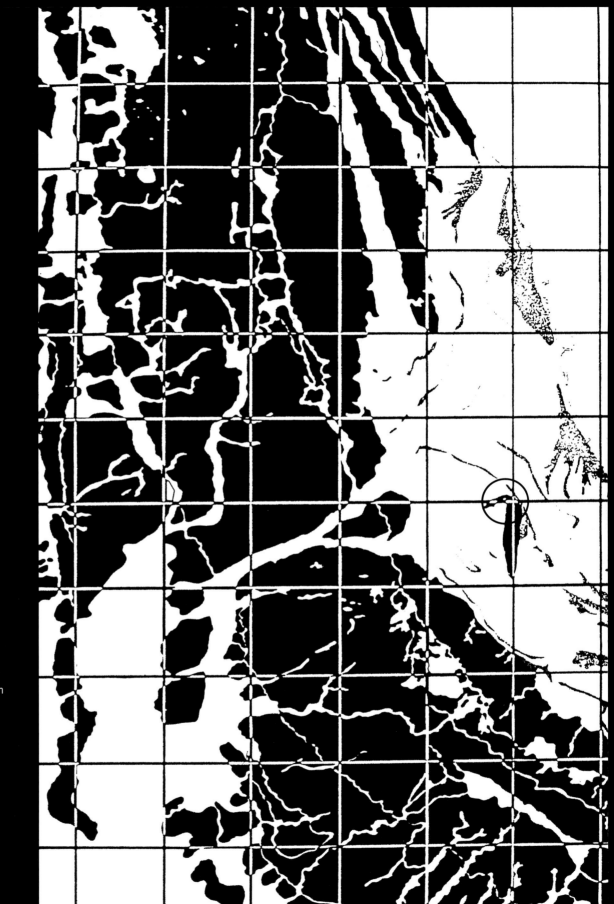

## TOPOGRAPHIC FRACTURE
## PLAN 1

The representation of the topographic changes in Chicago discloses a situation in which the isolated figure of a "whale" floating in the flat field next to Lake Michigan draws our attention acting as the "punctum" described by Roland Barthes in his writings on photography in the book *Camera Lucida*.

**PLAN 2**
A closer look reveals breaks and distortions of
the one-mile grid in the area adjacent to the
figure of the whale.

**PLAN 3**
The contrast between the complex configuration
of the jagged contour lines and the limited
effects on the one-mile grid express the power
of the latter as an ordering device.

**PLAN 4**
The abstract fictional representation of the thirty-
foot drop dramatizes the antagonism between
geography and the one-mile grid.

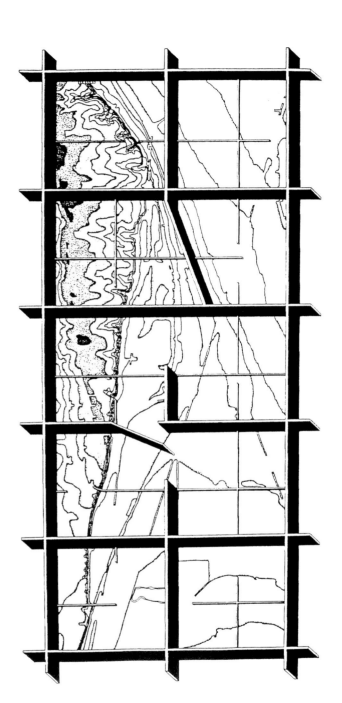
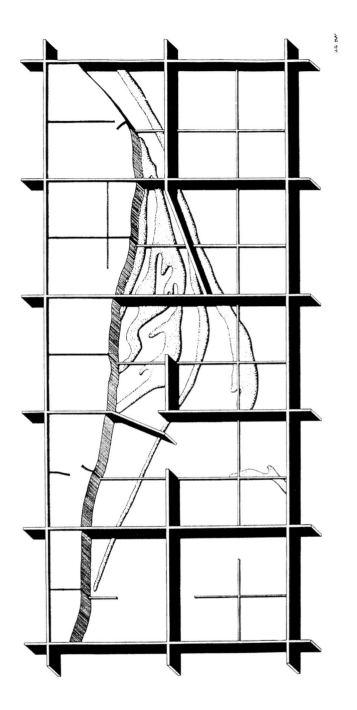

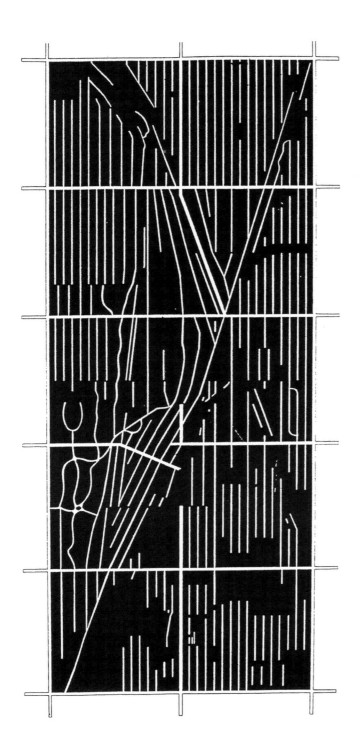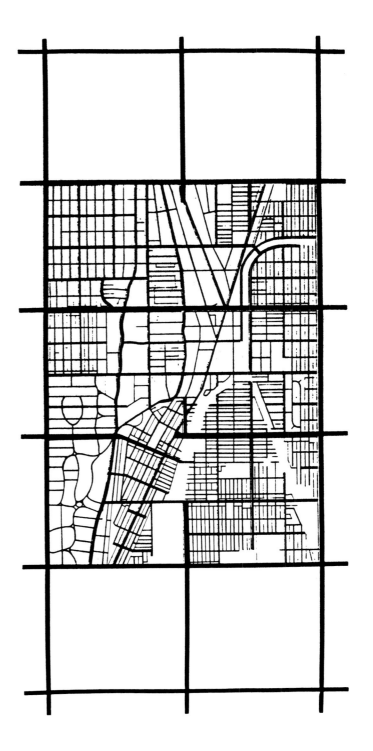

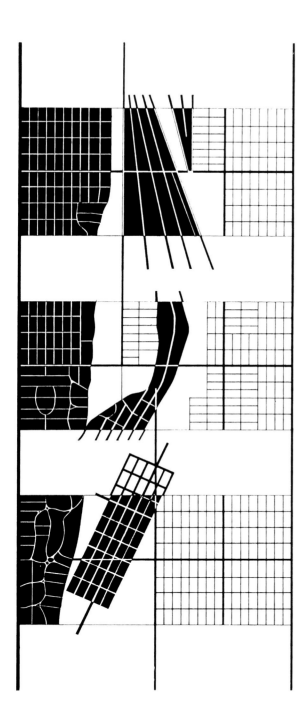

**PLAN 5**

The partial representation of the north-south streets shows the east-west fractures that translate the topographical irregularities into the logic of the structure of streets.

**PLAN 6**

The complete depiction of the streets shows the complex configurations that result from the different attempts to reestablish the continuity at the local level.

**PLAN 7**

Breaking the area in three sections allows us to depict the three different configurations that organize it: a grid, a group of streets converging to a nonextant center, and a mediating organic shape.

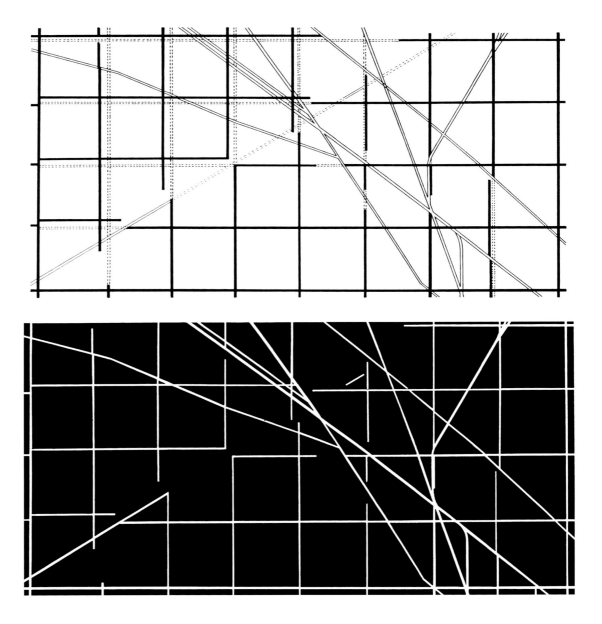

**PLAN 8**

The selected area, a four-by-eight sector of the one-mile grid, focuses on the effects of an area where several diagonals overlap: the diagonal dislocation of the one-mile grid.

**PLAN 9**

The drawing represents a major diagonal break and shift of the one-mile grid as well as minor breaks and shifts.

**PLAN 10**

The presence of the continuous ideal grid makes possible a more precise reading of the differential impact of the diagonals on the one-mile grid: from zero effect to a substantial jolt.

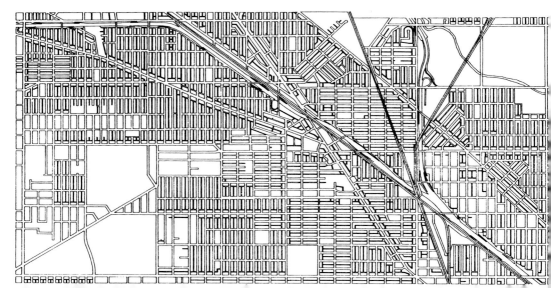

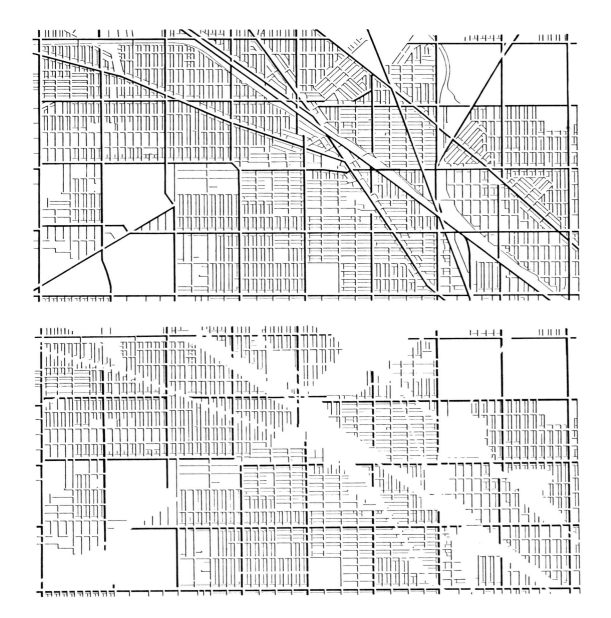

**PLAN 14**

The general effect in the area is seen in the change of the directionality of the fabric. The examination of the supposedly neutral square grid of streets reveals the existence of a double-street structure, in which a directionally biased structure of service alleys is concealed. The service alleys divide the square urban blocks into rectangular half-blocks, oriented sometimes along the north-south axis (parallel to the Lake Michigan coastline) and at other times along the east-west axis (perpendicular to the lake). This subdivision produces the reading of boundaries at the point where the service alleys change direction and therefore leads to the perception of a fracture of the fabric.

**PLAN 15**

A more detailed look at the fabric adjacent to the diagonals shows a distortion of the blocks and in some cases the emergence of a diagonal grid that is always contained within the boundaries of a square mile.

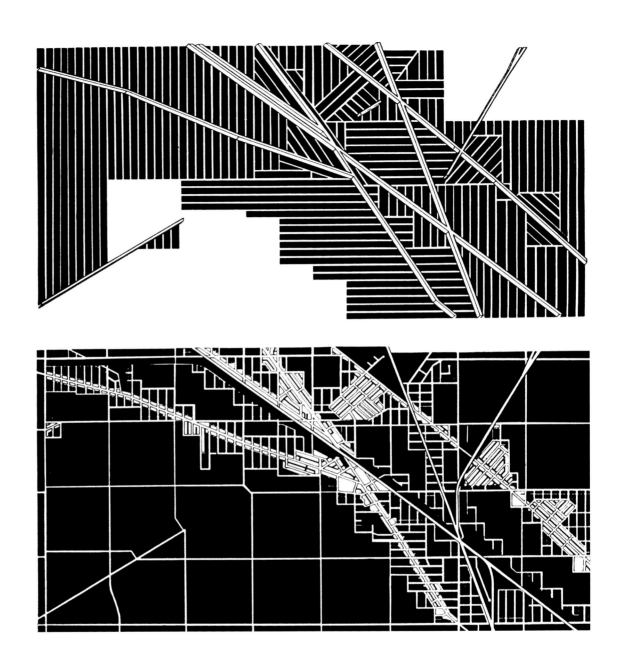

# THE COMPUTER DRAWINGS

**PLANS 1–4: BASIC ELEMENTS**
These four drawings describe the basic materials used in the computer studies of the Chicago plan: the street layout, the Chicago River, the one-mile grid, and the drawing that results from combining all three layers.

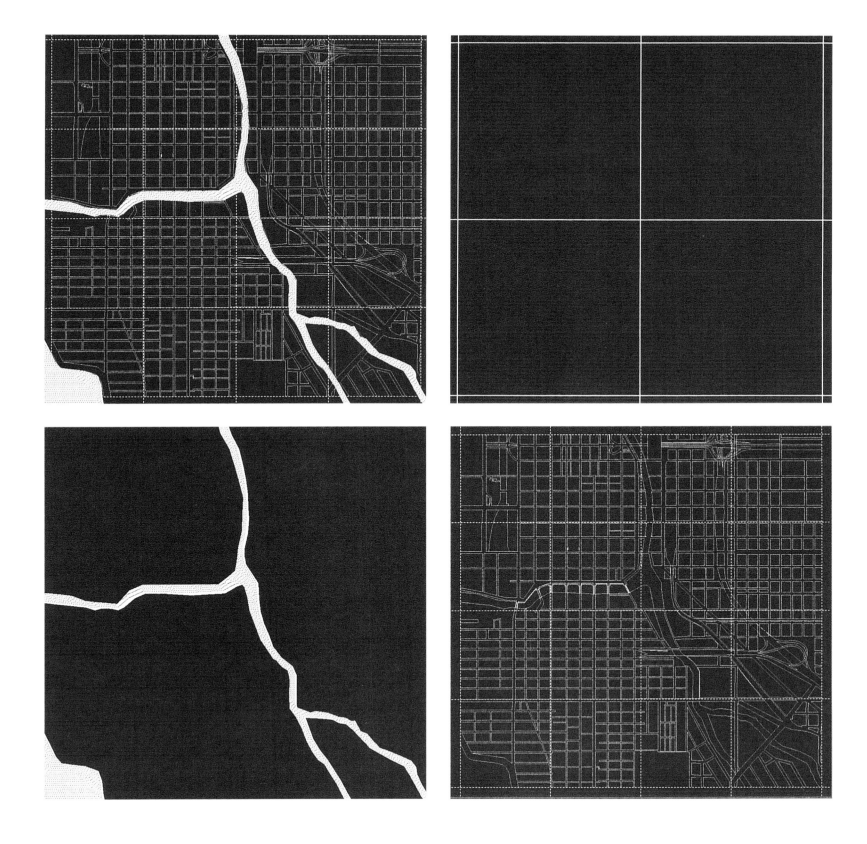

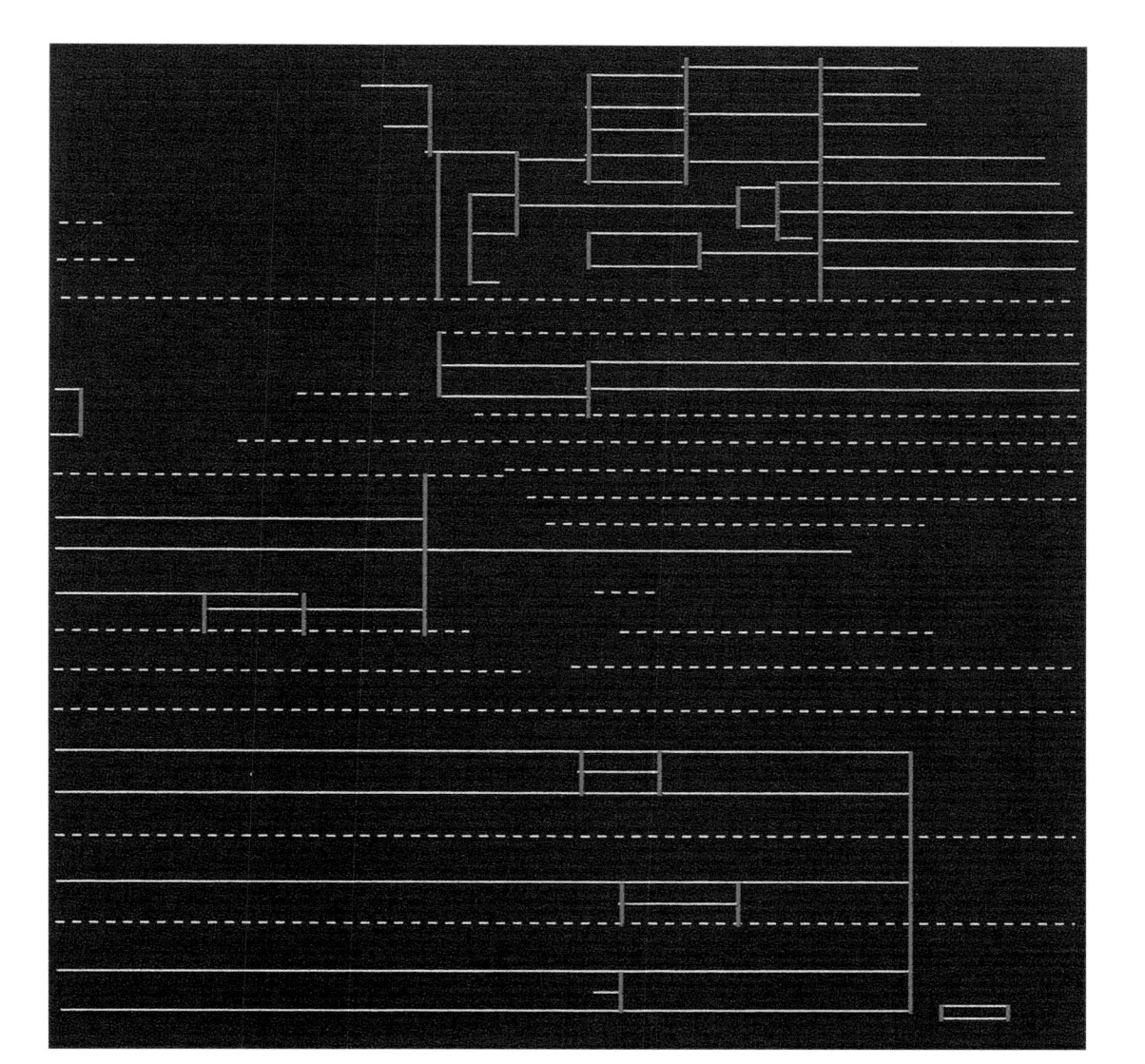

## PLANS 5-8:
### INVISIBLE WALLS

This series of drawings bring out an element that is not perceptible in the reality of the plan: the "invisible" walls. The layers depicting the horizontal and vertical streets show the "ghost" of the Chicago River in the breaks and discontinuities. However there are other breaks that do not relate to the river. Streets break, producing dead-ends and implying invisible walls that fragment the plan and produce districts that coincide with the public housing projects in the north, or separate white from black Chicago in the south.

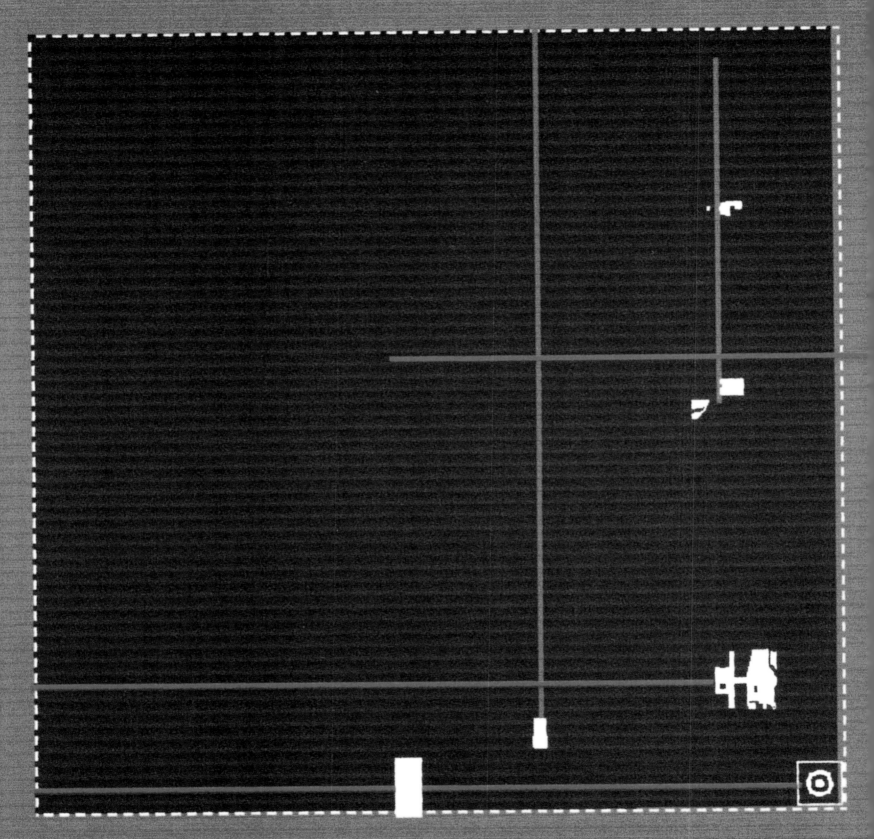

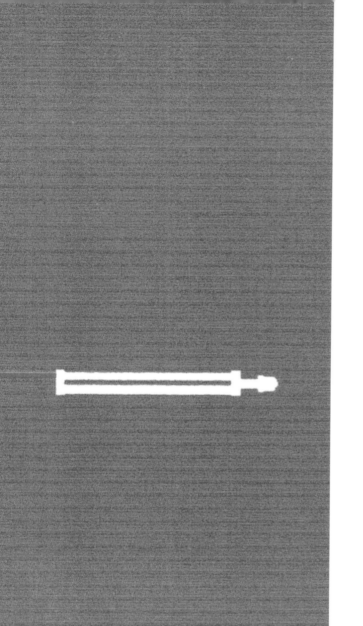

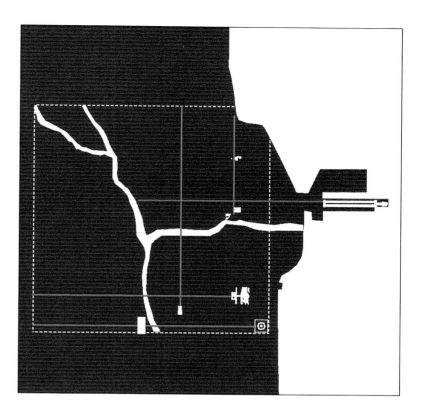

**PLANS 9–16:**

**THE READING OF THE LOOP**

This series of drawings is the only one where buildings, or more specifically plans of buildings, are included. The Loop appears structured by a square grid that is penetrated by an anomalous grid coming from the south. The drawings point to the static character of the neutral grid in contrast with the dynamic character of the directional grid. The next questions the drawings ask refers to the buildings in this area: Are they simply "fabric" or building-objects, or both? And how should they show the difference between the two conditions, between the extruded grids and the monuments? Fabric and building-objects seem to be the result of two inverse operations: while the fabric seems to respond to the forces of extrusion inherent to the grid, the building-objects seem to sit on the grid. A composition of lines and polygons describes the elements that escape the grid and its extrusion: the fabric. The polygons represent either building-objects detached from fabric or extrusions of entire city blocks, which defy or neutralize the opposition between fabric and building object. The lines represent the numerous alleys that do not belong to the grid. They depart from the perfect regularity of the ideal model. The series proposes a reading where the buildings seem to belong to two different structures: fabric or objects in a field. It implies the notion of the Loop (and perhaps the American city) as a field of building-objects overlapping the fabric of the city, or a twentieth-century city overlapping the nineteenth-century city.

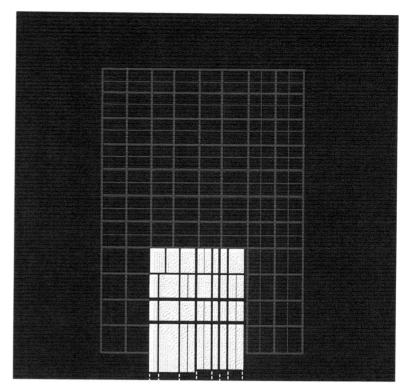

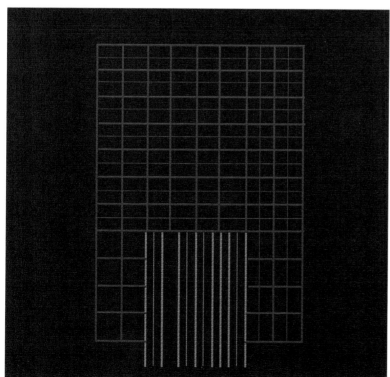

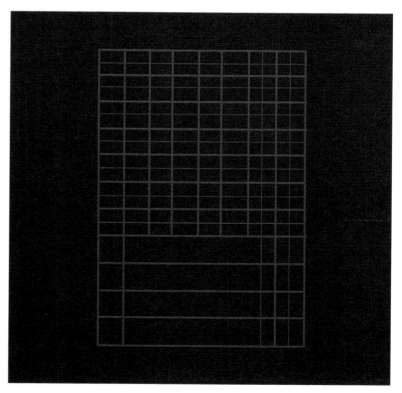

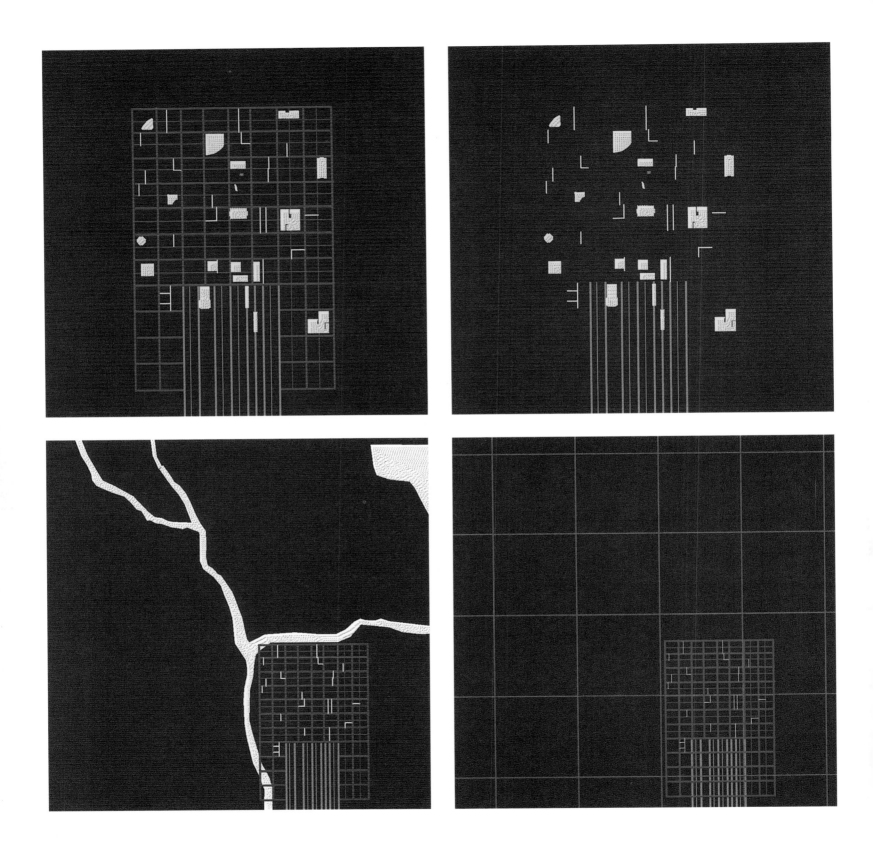

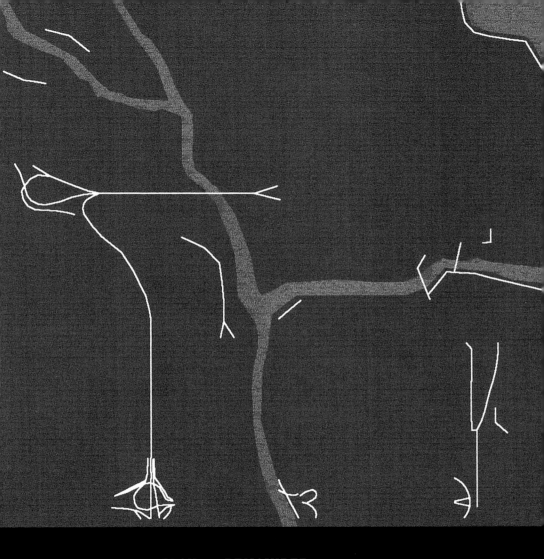

## PLAN 17: REMAINDER

Once we eliminate all the layers that produced the different narratives, we are left with the lines that resist narrativization. What do these lines represent? Freeway exits specifically, the absence of architecture generally

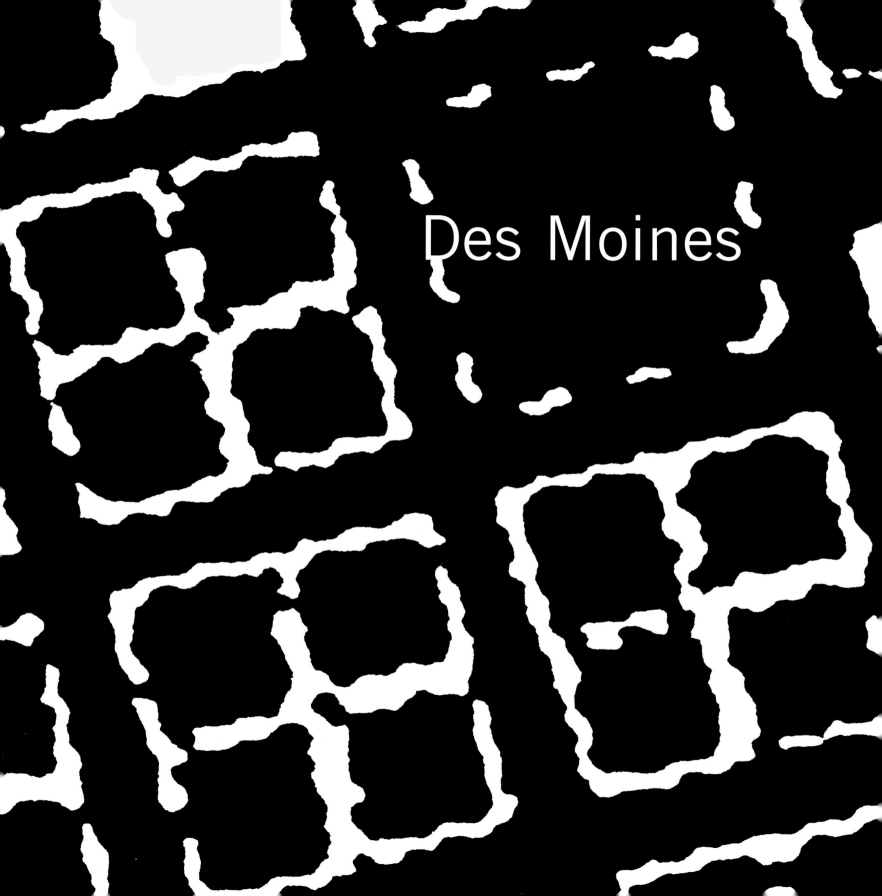

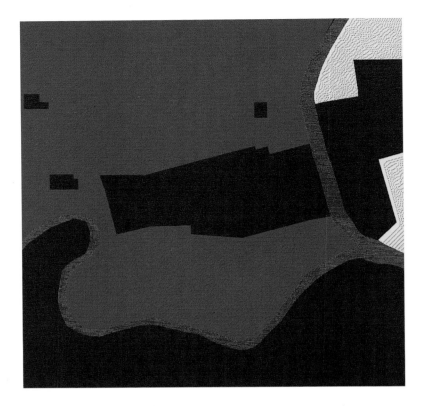
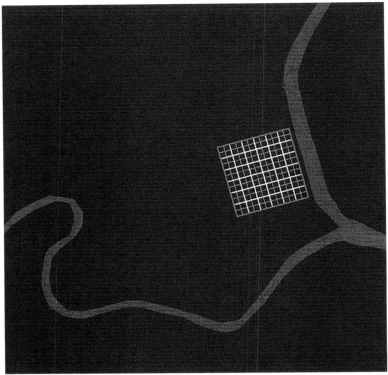
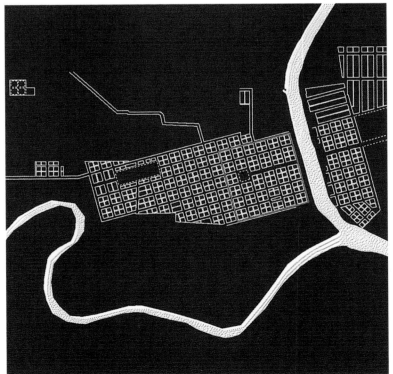
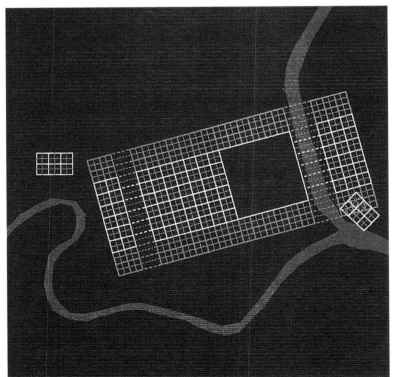

The urban significant moments play
against the background shaped by the conflicts
between the foundation grid,
the one-mile grid,
and the topographic irregularities.

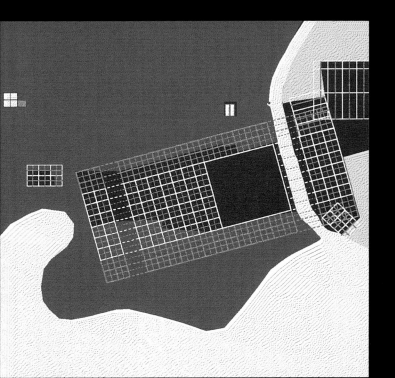

**PLANS 1-5:**
**THE FOUNDATION GRID**
The Des Moines foundation plan is established on an axis perpendicular to the Des Moines River. The original grid of six square blocks is extended to the west until it hits the Raccoon River and culminates to the east in the capitol grounds.

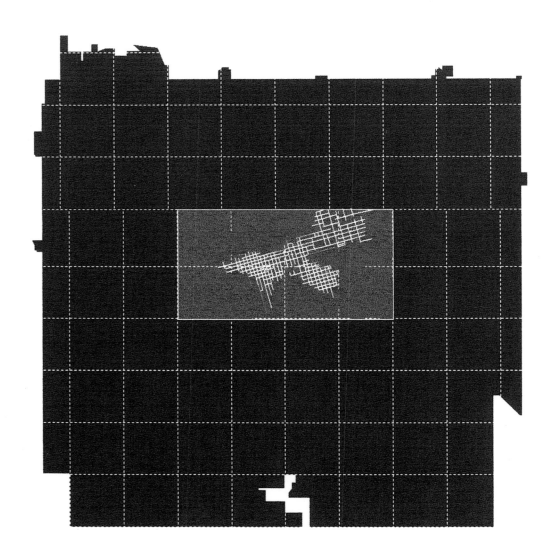

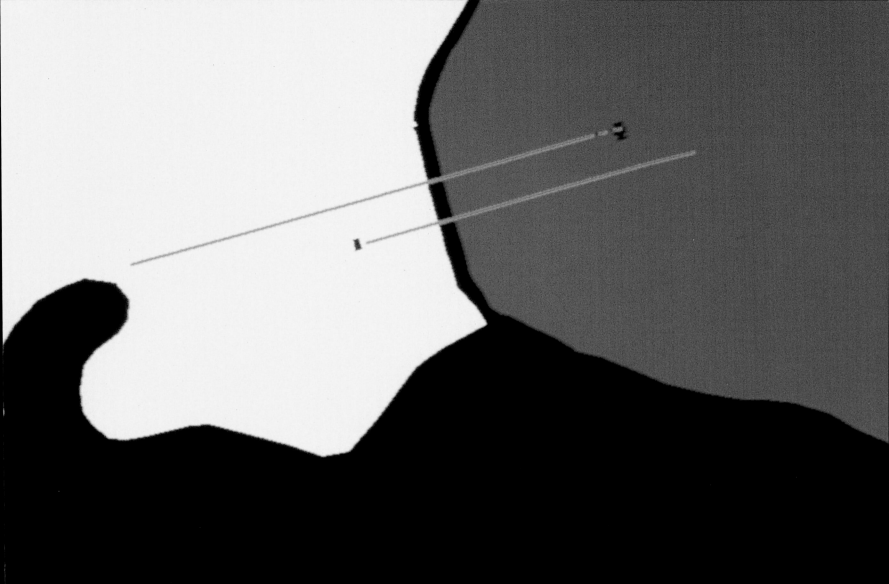

**PLAN 6:**
**THE TWO GRIDS**
The plan of Des Moines results from the juxtaposition and/or the interaction
of the original foundation grid and the north-south one-mile grid. A specific
formal feature of the plan results from the relationship between monuments
and streets within the original grid: the twin axes. Two other features result
from the interaction between grids: the Grand Avenue hinge linking the

**PLAN 7:**
**THE TWIN AXES**
Two streets dead-end on two major monuments: Locust Street at the state
capitol, located on the east side of the city, and Court Avenue at the court-
house, located on the west side. The streets imply a double movement and
reinforce the linear character of the downtown.

## PLAN 8:
## THE AVENUE HINGE

Grand Avenue is the only street that provides a strong transition between the two grids. It also intersects two important streets at the points of inflection: Fleur Drive and Hubell Avenue. It also links three major public places in Des Moines: the Des Moines Art Center at Greenwood Park on the west side, the fairgrounds on the east side, and the airport on the south side. (A fourth public space could potentially be located on Hubbell Avenue.) The points of inflection of change in direction represent potential gates into the city.

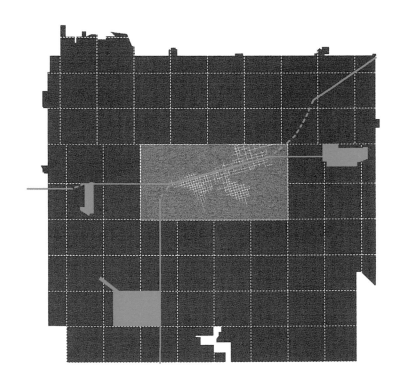

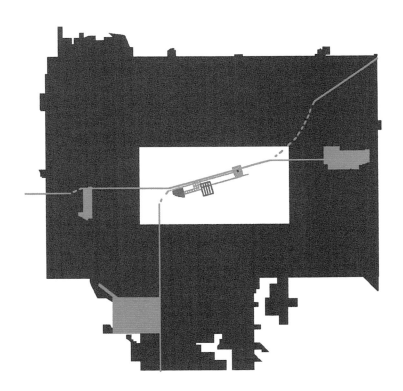

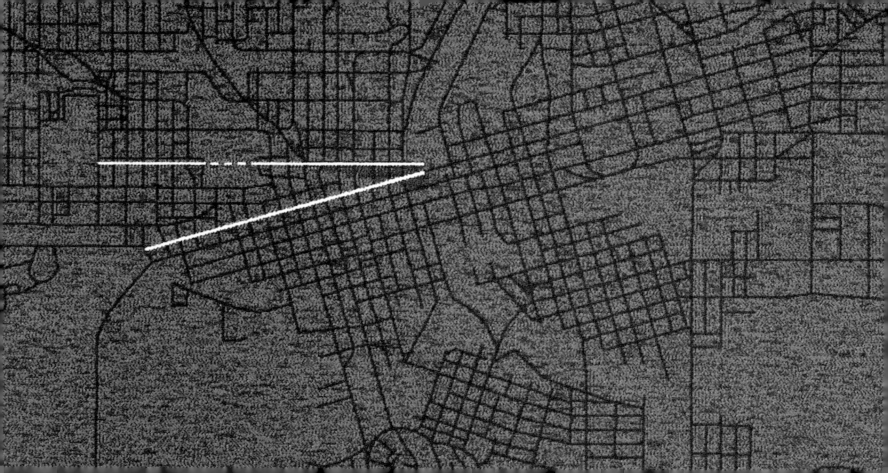

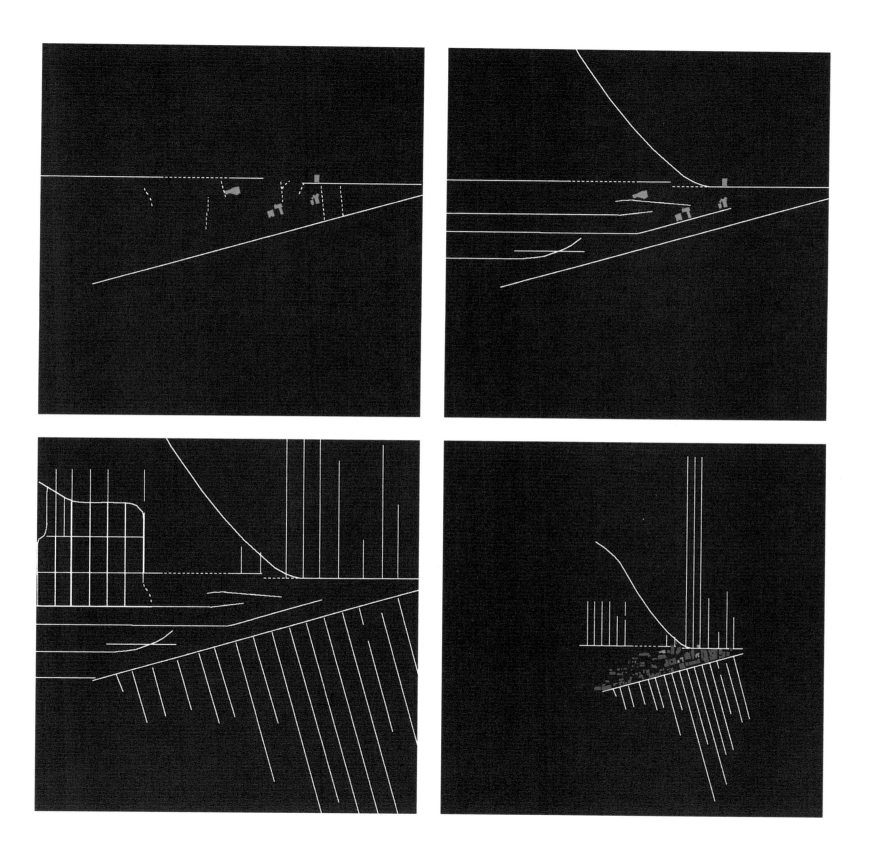

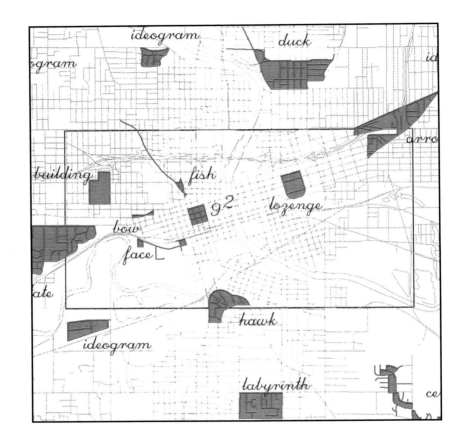

**PLANS 14-24:**

**THE TOPOGRAPHIC CONSTELLATIONS**

The distortions of the grid induced by the topography are read in their
figural implications, adding a mythological dimension to the plan.

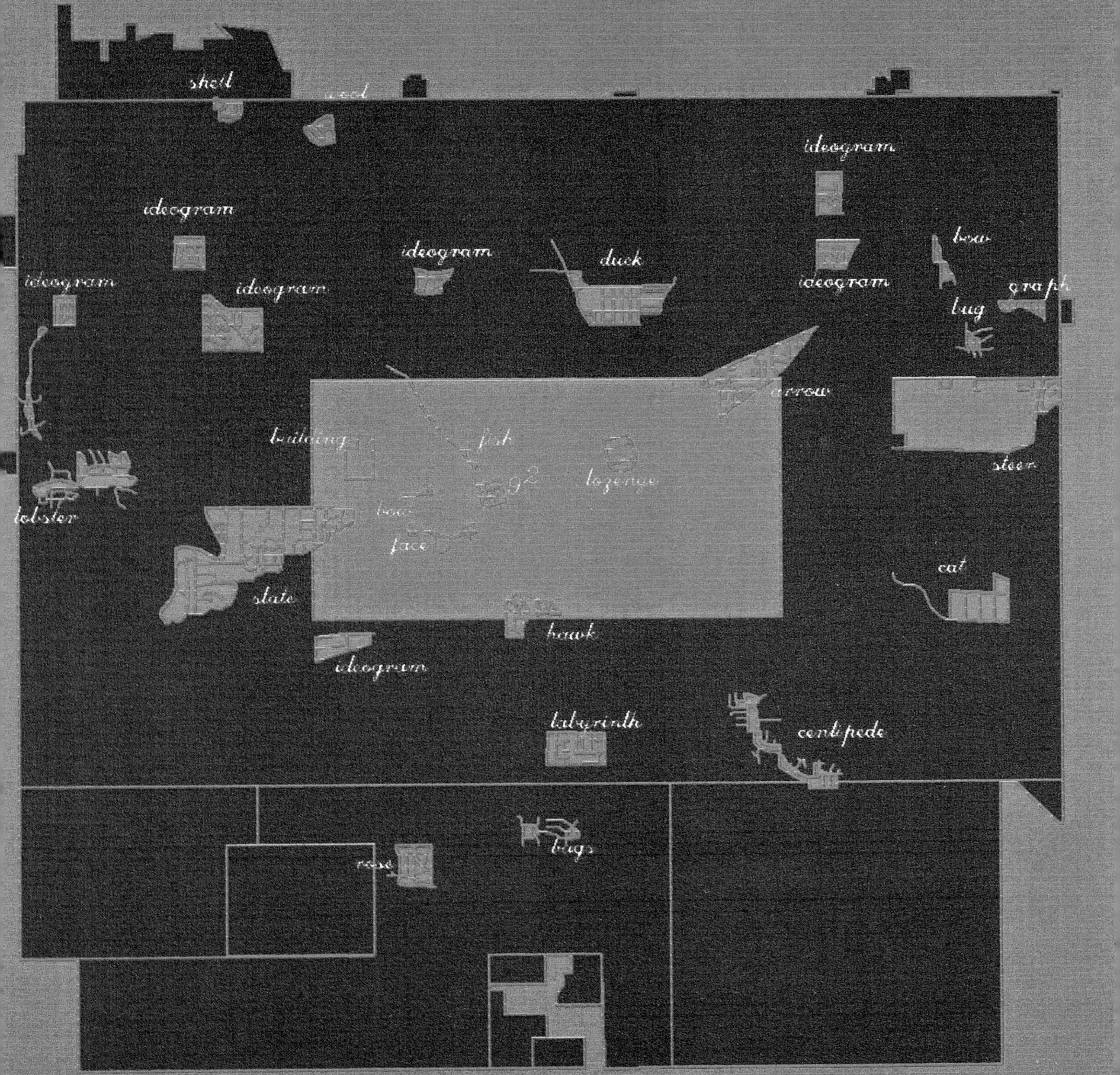

shell

reed

ideogram

ideogram

ideogram

ideogram

duck

box

graph

bug

ideogram

ideogram

arrow

building

fat

$g^2$

lozenge

steer

bow

face

lobster

cat

slate

hawk

ideogram

labyrinth

centipede

rose

bugs

*centipede*

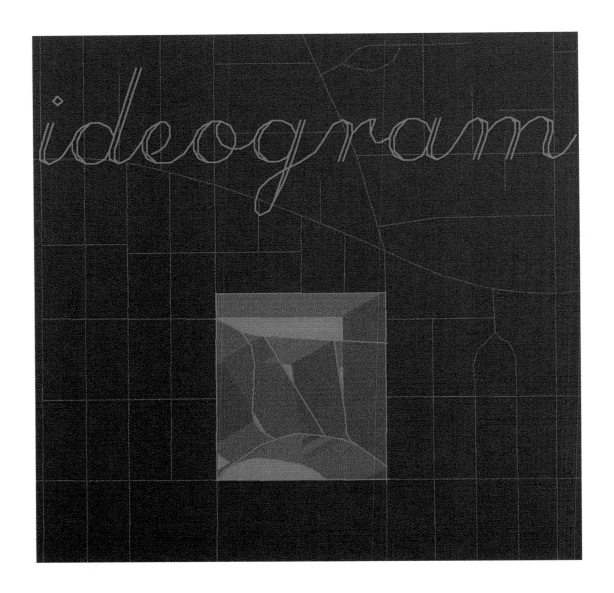

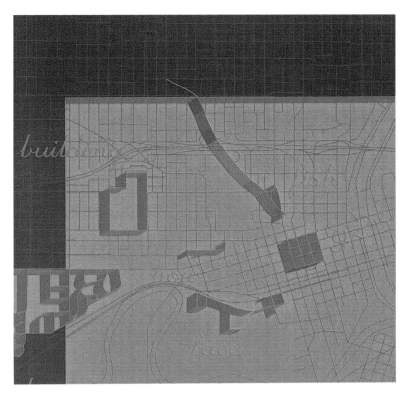
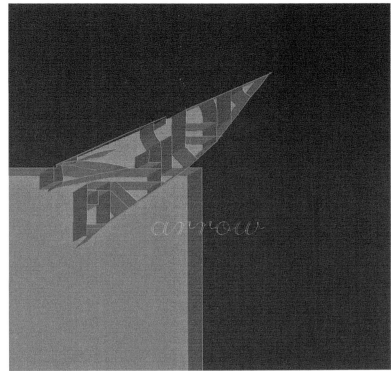
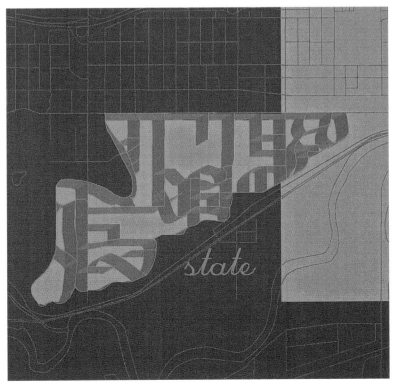

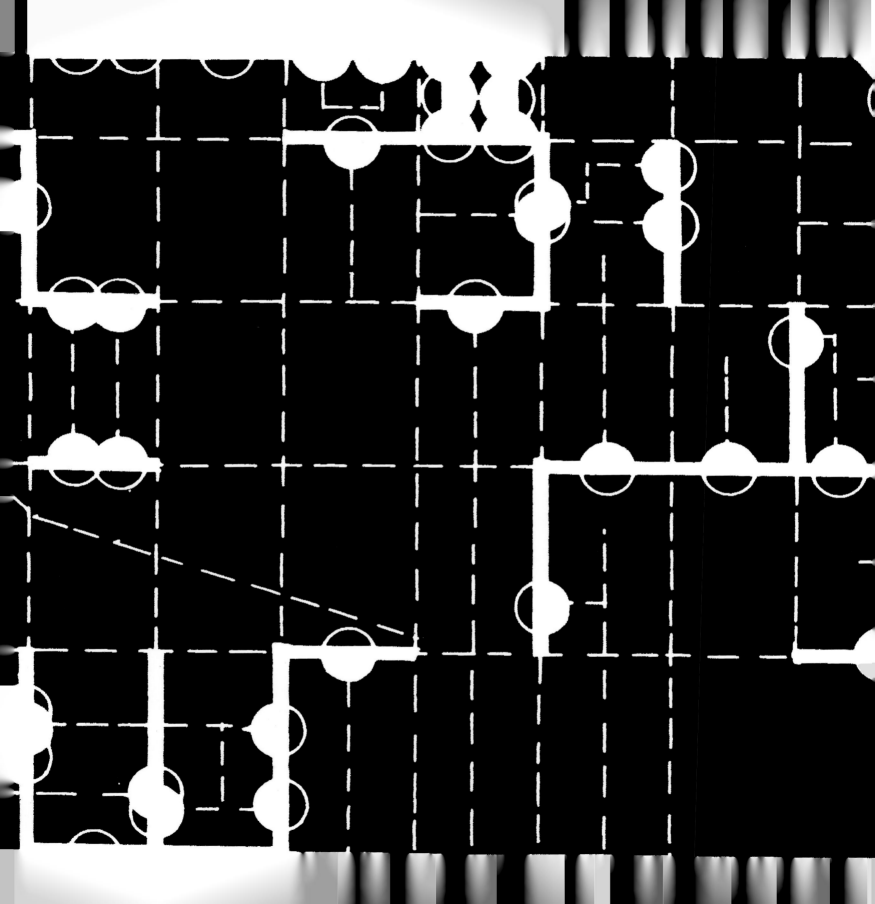

Atlantic City

The X-Urban erosion of the fabric
produces new constellations
of voids and solids.

PLANS 1-4:
**FRAGMENTATION OF THE GRID**
The early history of Atlantic City can be read in
the representation of the transformation of the
gridded plan, in the depiction of the fragmentation of the blocks defined by the streets.

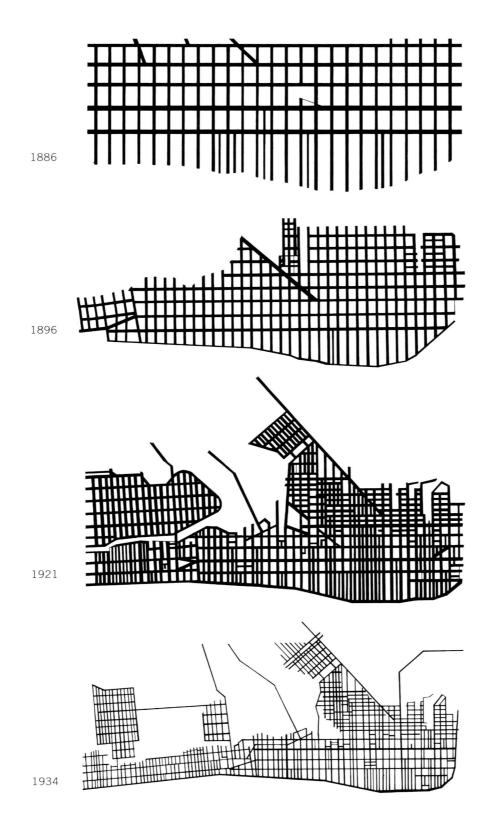

1886

1896

1921

1934

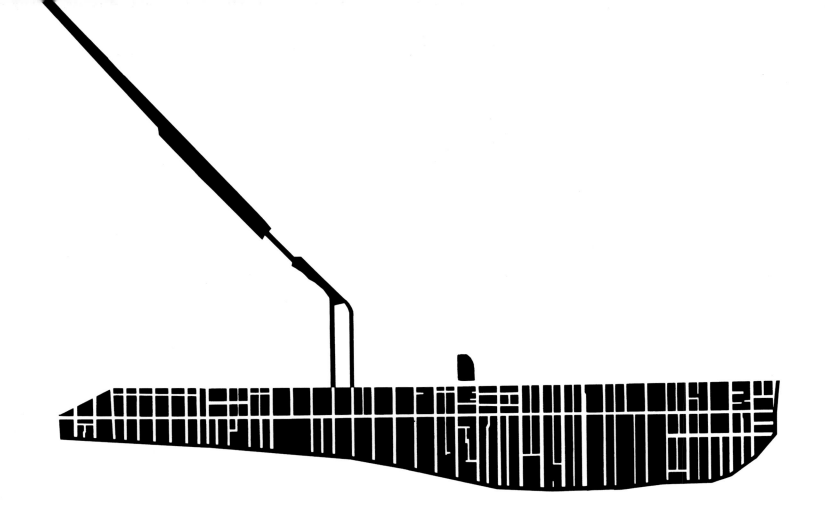

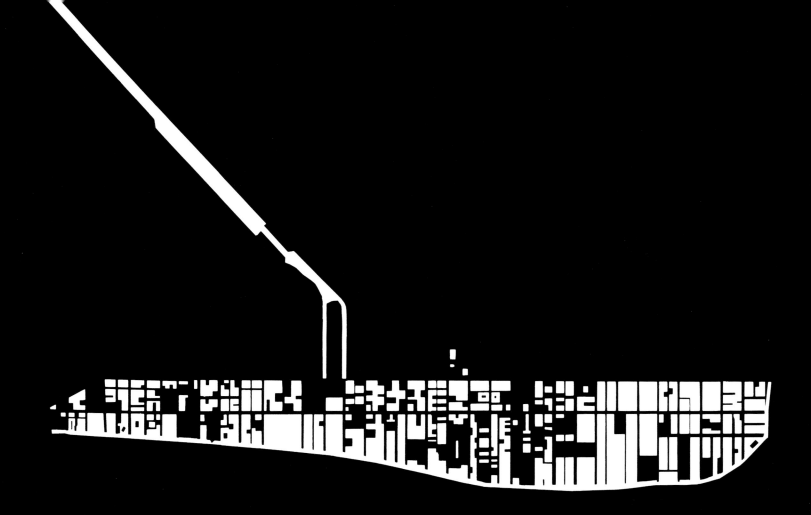

**PLANS 5-6:**

**THE SEA WALL**

The present condition shows a stage in the transformation of Atlantic City where Atlantic Avenue defines a wall that separates the positive growth of the sea wall. A wall made out of large object-buildings from the negative growth of the rest of the town, which is being demolished, remains as witnesses to the destruction isolated buildings or islands of fabric. The freeway dead-ends in this sea wall and erodes the fabric with parking structures.

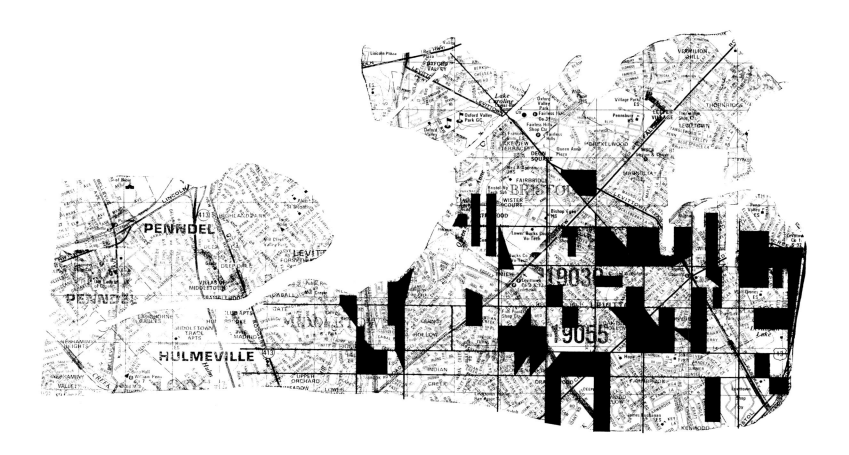

**PLANS 7-11:**

**ISLANDS OF FABRIC**

A series of fictional depiction takes the dead-ends as a point of departure
to identify the island of fabric seen as objects sitting on a field of asphalt or
rubble. The drawings deal with questions of directionality related to the
invisible walls and the degree of porosity that indicate the possibility of
future growth for the islands.

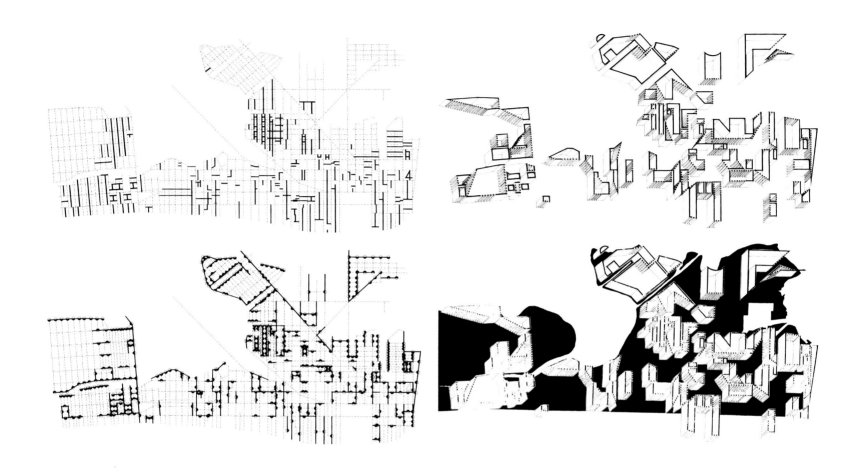

# Acknowledgments

I would like to mention those who helped the development of this book in different ways. First is Diana Agrest, for her enthusiastic support and for her pioneering work in the development of a poststructuralist urban theory and practice.

I am also grateful to the many schools that invited me to teach the seminars and studios where the first explorations on the American city took place and the students whose hard work and creativity were essential to the elaboration of this project. In 1983, Stanley Tigerman invited me to the School of Architecture at the University of Illinois to teach a studio where the questions presented in this book were first examined. The Institute for Architecture and Urban Studies provided the context for the development of the New York drawings, which were completed by a group of students led by one of my teaching assistants, Michael Stanton. In 1984, Frank Gehry arranged for me to come to the School of Architecture at University of Southern California, where students participated in the production of the Los Angeles drawings that were later developed in New York. I would like to give special mention to Christoph Kapeller, who created the final version of the Los Angeles drawings. Harry Cobb invited me to the Graduate School of Design at Harvard University, which provided the context for my first encounter with Boston. Cesar Pelli invited me to teach a studio at the School of Architecture at Yale University where the New Haven drawings were developed with Kevin Kennon as my teaching assistant. Rafael Moneo, Dean of the Graduate School of Design at Harvard University, invited me to teach the seminar where the Boston drawings published here were developed. In my undergraduate studio at the School of Architecture at Princeton University, the Atlantic City drawings were produced. Finally, I thank Antoine Grumbach at Unité Pedagogique 8, Belleville, and Jean-Louis Cohen at the Doctoral Program in Architecture in Paris for inviting me to teach the seminars to an European audience where some of the ideas presented in the book were tested.

Early versions of this book were given as conference papers or lectures. I am especially grateful to Ignasi Sola Morales, who invited me to participate in the planning of the UIA Congress of 1996, which provided a forum where partial versions of this text were presented. A Princeton University Council for the Humanities Grant enabled me to develop the Atlantic City drawings. John Whiteman, the first director of the Chicago Institute of Urbanism of the Skidmore, Owings & Merrill Foundation, invited me to be a fellow during the years 1988–90. Bruce Graham suggested the use of the computer. Julie Wheeler assisted in the production of the Chicago and Des Moines computer drawings, and Melva Bucksbaum introduced me to Des Moines. Kurt Forster invited me to the Getty Center where the research into early Los Angeles maps took place. The Maison Suger and its director Jean-Luc Lory provided, in Paris, the context for the revision of the final manuscript. Lucia Allais gave a thoughtful first reading of the text, and Julia Gandelsonas offered critical comments. Beth Harrison provided superb editorial work and leadership that kept everybody involved committed to the highest standards. Michael Rock contributed to the powerful graphic design guidelines, Sara Stemen created the design of the cover, and Dieter Janssen confronted a complex graphic design problem with elegant solutions.

# Index

# Illustration Credits

**PART 1**

Chapter 1

PAGE 13:  From John R. Spencer, trans., *Filarete's Treatise on Architecture*. New Haven, Conn.: Yale University Press, 1965.

PAGE 15:  (right) From Via Giulia, by Salerno, Spezzaferro, & Tafuri © Stabilimento Aristide Staderini spa Roma.
   (inset) From the Nolli plan of Rome, 1742, in Salerno, Spezzaferro, & Tafuri, Via Giulia © Stabilimento Aristide Staderini spa Roma.

PAGE 16:  St. Augustine, Florida (1556), early foundation plan. Unsigned, undated plan based on a survey by Don John de Solis drawn ca. 1770. From the Maps Division, Library of Congress, Washington D.C.
   Plan of Los Angeles, California. Untitled, undated manuscript copy of a plan showing Los Angeles, California, c. 1781. From the Bancroft Collection, University of California Library, Berkeley, California.
   Plan of New Haven, Connecticut. Drawn in 1748, by William Lyon. Published by T. Kensett, 1806. New-York Historical Society, New York, New York.
   Plan of Philadelphia, Pennsylvania. Drawn in 1682 by Thomas Holme, sold by Andrew Sowle. London, 1683. Olin Library, Cornell University, Ithaca, New York.
   (inset) View of Savannah, Georgia. Drawn in 1734, by Peter Gordon, London, England. Library of Congress, Prints and Photographs Division. Washington, D.C.

PAGE 17:  Drawing by G. F. Bordino, 1588.

PAGE 18:  (far left) Versailles: view of the chateau and garden,
   (left) Above Paris © Robert Cameron
   (right) From Melville C. Branch, *An Atlas of Rare City Maps*. New York: Princeton Architectural Press, 1997.

PAGE 19:  (left inset) From the series "Measures of Painting" by Albrecht Dürer.
   (right inset) From Jonathan Crary, *Techniques of the Observer: On Vision and Modernity in the Nineteenth Century*. Cambridge, Mass.: The MIT Press, 1991.

PAGE 20:  (inset) Drawn by Pierre Charles L'Enfant, 1791. From the collection of John Reps.

PAGE 21:  (top left) From Hildegard Binder Johnson, *Order upon the Land: The U.S. Rectangular Land Survey and the Upper Mississippi Country*.
   (top right) Drawn by Matthew Carey after surveys by Thomas Hutchins, published by Mathew Carey, Philadelphia, 1796. William L. Clements Library, University of Michigan, Ann Arbor, Michigan.

PAGE 21:  (inset) Photograph by Georg Gerster, 1990.

PAGE 22:  Photograph by Erich Mendelsohn © 1928.

PAGE 23:  (left) From Le Corbusier, *Urbanisme*. Paris: Èditions Vincent, Frèal & Co. Paris, 1924.
   (right) © Agrest 1974. From Diana Agrest, *Architecture From Without: Theoretical Framings for a Critical Practice*. Cambridge, Mass.: The MIT Press, 1991.

PAGE 24:  *From Techniques of the Observer: On Vision and Modernity in the Nineteenth Century*. Cambridge, Mass.: The MIT Press, 1991.

PAGE 25:  Copyright 1931 by Irving Underhill.

PAGE 26:  From Le Corbusier, *Urbanisme*. Paris: Èditions Vincent, Frèal & Co. Paris, 1924.

PAGE 27:  From Le Corbusier, *Urbanisme*. Paris: Èditions Vincent, Frèal & Co. Paris, 1924.

PAGE 28:  From Le Corbusier, *Urbanisme*. Paris: Èditions Vincent, Frèal & Co. Paris, 1924.

PAGE 29:  (left) From Le Corbusier, *Urbanisme*. Paris: Èditions Vincent, Frèal & Co. Paris, 1924.

PAGE 29:  (right) Mies van der Rohe: Lake Shore Drive, Chicago. 1951.

PAGE 30:  Photograph by Reyner Banham © 1971.

PAGE 31:  (left) © Fotofolio
   (right) © Fotofolio

PAGE 32:  Clarence Stein and Henry Wright. From Clarence Stein, *Toward New Towns for America*. Cambridge, Mass.: The MIT Press, 1966.

PAGE 33:  Courtesy of *The New York Times*, January 29, 1994.

PAGE 34:  (left) and (right) From Mellier Goodin Scott, *American City Planning Since 1890: A History Commemorating the Fiftieth Anniversary of the American Institute of Planners*. Berkeley:  University of California Press, 1969.

PAGE 35:  (left) From Werner Blaser, *Mies van der Rohe: The Art of Structure*. Zurich: Artemis Verlag und Verlag Für Architektur, 1965.

(right) From by Robert Venturi, Denise Scott Brown, and Steven Izenour, *Learning from Las Vegas*. Cambridge, Mass.: The MIT Press, 1972.

(inset) From Werner Blaser, *Mies van der Rohe: The Art of Structure*. Zurich: Artemis Verlag und Verlag Für Architektur, 1965.

PAGE 36:  Courtesy of Microsoft.

PAGE 37:  From Emmett Watson and Robert W. Cameron, *Above Seattle*. San Francisco: Cameron & Co., 1994.

PAGE 38:  Photograph by Jeff Perkell.

PAGE 39:  (inset) From *Cesar Pelli: Buildings and Projects 1965–1990*. New York: Rizzoli, 1990.

(right) Courtesy of Mario Gandelsonas.

PAGE 41:  (inset) © 1998 Matt McCourt and Carl Dahlman, as first published in *The Atlantic Monthly*, July 1998.

PAGE 42:  Photograph by Alex S. MacLean. From James S. Corner, Alex S. MacLean (photographer), and Denis Cosgrove, *Taking Measures Across the American Landscape*, New Haven, Conn.: Yale University Press, 1996.

PAGE 43:  Photograph by Alex S. MacLean. From James S. Corner, Alex S. MacLean (photographer), and Denis Cosgrove, *Taking Measures Across the American Landscape*, New Haven, Conn.: Yale University Press, 1996.

CHAPTER 2

PAGE 46:  Drawn ca. 1855 by Asselineau from a watercolor painting by John Bachman, published by Wild, Paris, France. From the Maps Division, Library of Congress, Washington, D.C.

PAGE 47:  (left) from John Summerson, *Georgian London*. London: Barrie & Jenkins, 1988.

(center) From *Le Petit Atlas Maritime by Belin*, Olin Library, Cornell University, Ithaca, New York.

(right) Drawn by Abbè Delagrive, Paris, 1746. From the collection of John Reps.

PAGE 50:  Map published by J. J. Stoner, 1882. From the Maps Division, Library of Congress, Washington, D.C.

PAGE 51:  (right) From Aymonino, Fabbri, and Villa, *Le Citt Capitali del XIX Secolo* © 1975.

(left) Drawing of Washington, D.C., developed by Erika Schmitt in the context of Mario Gandelsonas's seminar, *The Urban Text*, at the School of Architecture, Princeton University.

PAGE 52:  From Giorgio Ciucci, Francesco Dal Co, Manieri Elia, and Manfredo Tafuri, *The American City: From the Civil War to the New Deal*. Cambridge, Mass.: The MIT Press, 1979.

PAGE 53:  From Giorgio Ciucci, Francesco Dal Co, Manieri Elia, and Manfredo Tafuri, *The American City: From the Civil War to the New Deal*. Cambridge, Mass.: The MIT Press, 1979.

PAGE 54:  From Giorgio Ciucci, Francesco Dal Co, Manieri Elia, and Manfredo Tafuri, *The American City: From the Civil War to the New Deal*. Cambridge, Mass.: The MIT Press, 1979.

PAGE 55:  (left) Asher B. Durand, Dover Plain, Duchess County, New York, 1848.

PAGE 56:  (left) From *Toward New Towns for America*, by Clarence Stein © 1957.

(inset) Photograph by Walter Gropius.

CHAPTER 3

PAGE 69:  (bottom) *The Master's Bedroom* © 1920 Max Ernst.

## PART 2

Chapter 4

PAGES 82–97:  The New York drawings were developed by
the students of Mario Gandelsonas's undergraduate studio at
the Institute for Architecture and Urban Studies in 1983–84.
The final renderings were produced by Michael Stanton,
one of the teaching assistants, with Nancy Clayton and Alan
Organsky. The drawings on pages 88–9 were developed by
I. K. Bun.

PAGES 100–9:  The Los Angeles drawings were developed by
the students in Mario Gandelsonas's seminar on Los Angeles
at the School of Architecture, University of Southern
California, in the fall of 1984. The final renderings were
produced in New York by Kristoph Kapeller in the summer
of 1985.

PAGES 112–9:  The Boston drawings were developed by
students in Mario Gandelsonas's seminar on Boston at the
Graduate School of Design, Harvard University, in the fall
of 1986.

PAGES 123–9:  The New Haven drawings were developed by
students in Mario Gandelsonas's fall 1987 graduate studio,
with Kevin Kennon as the teaching assistant.

PAGES 133–53:  The Chicago ink drawings were developed
by students in Mario Gandelsonas's seminar on Chicago at
the School of Architecture, University of Illinois. The author

would like to make special mention of Julie Evans (pages
132–7) and Brendan Fahey (pages 138–43). The Chicago
computer drawings were developed by Mario Gandelsonas
at the Chicago Institute for Architecture and Urbanism in
1988–9 with the assistance of Julie Wheeler.

PAGES 156–71:  The Des Moines computer drawings were
developed by Mario Gandelsonas at the Chicago Institute for
Architecture and Urbanism in 1989–91 with the assistance of
Julie Wheeler.

PAGES 175–81:  The Atlantic City drawings were developed by
the students of Mario Gandelsonas's undergraduate studio at
the School of Architecture, Princeton University.